METHODS IN SOCIAL AND EDUCATIONAL CARING

Methods in Social and Educational Caring

Edited by
JOHN McGREGOR McMASTER
University of Newcastle upon Tyne

Gower

Published by

Gower Publishing Company Limited,
Gower House, Croft Road,
Aldershot, Hants GU11 3HR, England

British Library Cataloguing in Publication Data

Methods in social and educational caring.
1. Problem children
2. Child psychotherapy
I. McMaster, John McGregor
618.92'89'14 RJ504

ISBN 0 566 00386 4 (cased edition)
ISBN 0 566 00578 6 (limp edition)

Printed in Great Britain by
Biddles Ltd, Guildford, Surrey

Contents

Preface

This is the first of two books on social and educational caring. For many years I have been interested in the problems of children and young people. I have also been interested in their treatment. Working with social workers, teachers, doctors, psychiatrists, psychologists, therapists and parents convinces me that most problems are of common professional concern. The concept of multi-disciplinary treatment and professional integration is exciting, desirable, but difficult to put into practice.

Practice inevitably involves *methods* and this text examines five which are current and controversial: assessment, behaviour modification, intermediate treatment, the therapeutic community and group work.

John McGregor McMaster
University of Newcastle upon Tyne
March 1982

List of contributors

John D. Begg

Trained initially as a probation officer, John Begg has been working with children and young people for over twenty years in a caring capacity.

He is currently Deputy Head of a Scottish List 'D' School which has an experimental approach to children in trouble. He has been involved in many working parties and has recently been engaged in research on the concept of the Therapeutic Community.

John McGregor McMaster

Lecturer in Behavioural Science, University of Newcastle upon Tyne. Formerly Senior Lecturer in Educational Psychology and Senior Tutor at Preston Polytechnic. Has undertaken evaluative research for IBM in simulation and gaming in schools in the N.E. of England.

Evaluator for experimental course organised by DES for teachers and social workers in 1977 and 1978. Consultant to a number of voluntary and statutory organisations. Co-tutor to the B.Phil. in residential care and education at the University of Newcastle upon Tyne. Author of *Toward an Educational Theory for the Mentally Handicapped*, Edward Arnold, 1973.

Contributor, reviewer and referee to a number of journals and periodicals. External examiner to courses in education *and* social work, at first professional and post-professional level. Research interests include microtraining, behaviour modification and behavioural difficulties in children and young people. Frequent lecturer at national conferences. Especially interested in an integrated and multi-disciplinary approach for the caring professions.

William S. More

Currently Principal Lecturer and Director of Studies, Department of Sociology and Applied Social Studies, Birmingham Polytechnic. Formerly Principal, Royal Caledonian School, Herts.

Leverhulme Research Fellow 1974-1976 during which he produced 'An Evolving Therapeutic Community'. Research Officer, Priority Educational Programmes for Action and Research in the areas of Home Teaching, School Rejection and Intermediate Treatment.

Research Director, National Intermediate Treatment Study, 1977-1978. Consultant to Northern Ireland Office for Development of Intermediate Treatment. Contributor to many periodicals and journals.

Author of *Emotions and Adult Learning*, Saxon House 1974.

Denis J. O'Connor

Tutor to advanced degree and diploma courses at University of Newcastle upon Tyne. Formerly head of Education Department in a College of Education. Has a wide experience of directing in-service training courses for senior staff for both the education and social services. Currently evaluating a short staff training module for the DHSS and is organising an experimental inter-disciplinary in-service training course for teachers and social workers for a local Health Education Authority. External examiner to a number of degree courses and contributor regularly to journals and periodicals.

Presently consultant psychologist and psycho-therapist to voluntary and statutory organisations.

Director of a university counselling clinic for adolescents suffering behaviour disorders.

Current research interests include simulated social skills training, drug, alcohol and solvent abuse.

Jack B. Ronaldson

Tutor to MSc course in Educational Psychology at University of Newcastle upon Tyne. Formerly educational psychologist with a number of LEAs.

Currently involved as a consultant psychotherapist to a number of organisations and institutions in the North East of England. Contributor to journals and periodicals, his research interests include group dynamics, adolescence and children with behavioural difficulties. Works extensively with different professional groups, for example, social workers, teachers, youth and community workers, psychologists and psychiatrists.

Acknowledgements

My thanks to the contributors, Denis O'Connor, William More, John Begg and Jack Ronaldson.

My gratitude to Patricia MacDonald for material in chapter 4 and to Joe Westmorland for material in chapter 2.

I am grateful to my secretary Olive Carrott for co-operation and advice at various stages in the planning, writing and typing of the manuscript. My thanks to Susan Holliday and Doreen Edwards for excellent typing under a great deal of pressure.

Finally, my thanks to my wife for her professional guidance, assistance and unfailing enthusiasm.

J.McG.McM.

1 Method: an introduction
JOHN McGREGOR McMASTER

This book should be helpful to teachers and social workers. It should also be of interest to others in the 'caring professions', e.g. psychologists, psychiatrists, youth and community workers.

It examines five methodological approaches which are pertinent to problems in social and educational caring. These approaches are: assessment, behaviour modification, intermediate treatment, the therapeutic community and group work.

Teachers and social workers are key figures in this area and their responsibility is great. Consider the following real examples:

> Ann is 10 years old. Her behaviour is causing concern at school. She is apathetic and withdrawn from the other children in class and from her teacher. It is well known that the home is dirty, impoverished and it is suspected that Ann may be being physically abused by the parents. The family have had considerable contact with social workers in the past and Ann is currently the focal point of a social worker's investigation. Clearly Ann needs care both social and educational.

> Brian is 13 years of age. His parents have separated and custody has been given to the mother. Financial difficulties have become acute and the social worker is concerned about the mental health of the mother and the effect upon the child. There has been sudden deterioration in Brian's subject performance in school,

from above average to borderline ESN. He has also become increasingly aggressive. The psychologist's report shows a score of 115 on the Wechsler Intelligence Scale for Children, above average. Brian is a problem. A social problem and an educational problem.

A teacher in a large primary and middle school states that 60 per cent of the children in his class usually come to school without breakfast and without adequate sleep. A social worker is involved with more than half; social and educational problems abound.

Social work and teaching are, mainly, problem-solving activities and it would seem logical to look at methods which help towards solution of the problems. There are a number of reasons for the selection of the methodological approaches referred to just now.

1 Teachers and social workers are concerned with learning situations for their children and clients. They are involved in bringing about *change* in behaviour patterns and this should mean a focus upon methods. The five areas selected are of common interest to teachers and social workers; both professional groups can be *active* participants.

2 The five areas are current, controversial and each will be subject to increased scrutiny and development in the 1980s.

3 The areas have evolved from a mixture of experience, experimentation, research and legislation.

4 The author has personal experience as teacher, social worker, tutor, and external examiner. In this latter capacity examining courses in teacher training *and* social work has been invaluable.

Assessment

There is an increase in the recognition of the importance of assessment, even though, under examination and scrutiny, the constitution of assessment varies enormously. In education and social work there is constant reference by working parties and commissions to the need for assessment of children. The teacher in the classroom is expected to undertake some form of assessment of the child's ability and progress; the social worker makes an assessment of clients and situations. If one examines syllabuses of courses in the caring professions it can be seen that they emphasise the importance of assessment.

This insistence on the importance of assessment makes it even more pressing to attempt some examination of the elements which make up assessment. Many of these elements can be classed as methods in themselves.

In recent years, teachers, social workers, psychiatrists, psychologists and others have hotly debated the relationship between assessment, treatment, therapy and education. This has been noticeable at conferences organised by DES, DHSS and professional associations. A typical example is, on the one hand, the view that assessment should be separate from treatment; on the other that to separate assessment from treatment is an artificial division which can only result in inferior provision for the child. By examining the concept of assessment and its practice it can be shown that assessment as a method varies greatly. Awareness of this helps eradicate spurious disagreements.

There is a danger of assessment taking place in a vacuum or data becoming an end in itself. At this point assessment ceases to be helpful and contrary to the very nature of education and social work. The compilation of data for its own sake and not that of the child is a sterile exercise.

Methods of assessment fall into three categories:

1 *Formal assessment methods* including factual data on the child, results of standardised tests, e.g. intelligence tests and attainment tests.

2 *Semi-formal assessment methods* containing rating scales, schedules and reports where some standardised format exists.

3 *Informal assessment methods* including impressionistic reports of a subjective nature.

Chapters 2 and 3 examine some problems in these categories.

Behaviour modification

It is unfortunate that much of the writing on behaviour modification is highly technical and suggests a cold and mechanical approach to human behaviour. Add to this the inevitable superficial stereotype derived from early animal experiments and it is easy to understand the rejection by many in the caring profession who believed that behaviour modification was eliminating emotion and cognition. This is not so and the efficiency of the method is such that, provided the skill is there, behaviour modification has enormous potential in the area of human learning. Given that teachers and social workers are in the business of *changing* behaviour then it is reasonable to look for effective and efficient methods. An ethical evaluation of the objectives specified by the teacher or social worker is not the prerogative of behaviour modification, or indeed its parent discipline, psychology. It is to philosophy one must look for some solution to that problem. Having made this point, most people would agree on major areas of desirable and undesirable behaviour. To this end behaviour modification is critically important because of its power as a method.

In chapter 4 the intention is to give the reader an introduction to behaviour modification as a method and, it is hoped, an introduction which will allow him to see its immediate relevance to everyday behavioural acts. The literature abounds with sophisticated and detailed examples of programmes which give the impression of behavioural straitjackets. This need not be the case; behaviour modification can be a method which assists us towards freedom and creativity. Chapter 5 describes behaviour modification in action. The examples are deliberately simple since the intention is to show that application can be achieved quickly and effectively within a very short time span.

Intermediate treatment

This is a term which is now firmly part of the vocabulary of many in the caring professions, and especially in social work. This would suggest that, as a method, and one which has been running for more than a decade, it should be readily defined and easily understood. Not only that, we could understandably look for evidence of its efficacy.

William More shows us in chapter 6 that much confusion surrounds the concept of intermediate treatment. His examples and definitions make us wonder whether it has established itself as a distinct method. But central and local government have invested time and money in intermediate treatment schemes. It would, therefore, seem essential that those concerned with the care and education of young people should know precisely what stage intermediate treatment has reached as a method.

Labels often assume overtones of respectability in the context of a professional vocabulary and this is so with intermediate treatment. Unfortunately, this presupposes a common knowledge which is sometimes absent. Frequently, social workers, teachers, magistrates, probation officers and others do interpret intermediate treatment differently. This emphasises the need for a clear exposition. Implicit is much that is desirable including many of the elements which are currently being advocated in social work and education. Not the least of these is the inter-professional and inter-disciplinary function which intermediate treatment as method could achieve. As William More says, '12 years on intermediate treatment is at a crossroads'. It is to be hoped that the direction it will take will result in a well articulated method with a clearly formulated rationale.

Therapeutic community

This is another good example of a term which, if taken literally, would simply mean some form of treatment in a community setting. Such a definition would apply to all 'group' situations from the family through the school to various institutions and establishments. But terms and labels often assume different connotations in a professional context and this is the case with the therapeutic community which has definite parameters. It may seem strange to take a method which was originally developed and established as treatment for psychiatric patients in a hospital setting and include it as a major method in this text. There are very sound reasons for its inclusion.

The therapeutic community is a form of groupwork and the establishments in which it is practised operate very much on the basis of the 'group' forming the main vehicle for education or treatment. Maxwell Jones, who was largely responsible for the development of the therapeutic community, makes the point that, 'The Therapeutic Community is distinctive among the comparable treatment centres in the way the institution's total resources, both staff and patients, are self-consciously pooled in furthering treatment' (Jones, 1959).

This approach has become associated with establishments for children and young people with some form of problem behaviour or educational need. In some ways, looking back, A.S. Neill could be associated with a type of therapeutic community. The four main characteristics which make up the method are: democratisation, permissiveness, communalism, and reality confrontation.

The therapeutic community method has its vociferous supporters and vehement critics. Many professionals in care and education are concerned because the method is increasingly being adopted by young people with insufficient experience and knowledge. This is dangerous. Perhaps the most obvious feature to the visitor would be the 'community meeting' in which the individual's problems are discussed openly by the group. Independent observers of these meetings are often in disagreement about their efficacy.

Groupwork

In the last 30 years, there has been much experimentation in the use of groups. Groupwork as a method is important since participants can be students, delinquents, priests, teachers, social workers, youth leaders, police officers, executives – the list is almost endless. Many people have experienced groupwork as sensitivity training in some form, without realising how it developed. Sensitivity training, or the 'T' group as it is often referred to, sprang from research begun by Kurt Lewin. One reason for the instigation of the 'T' group was the concern over leadership roles in the second world war 1939-1945. This was related to the incredible power of autocratic leadership exhibited by Hitler and others. Lewin wished to help people to become more effective in democratic functioning. The main aims of groupwork would seem admirable: increasing awareness of perception of self and others; increasing sensitivity to what other people are thinking and feeling; increasing communication of feeling; and increasing more effective group functioning. These aims would not be disputed by many. One problem, and a large one, is whether the 'T' group achieves these aims. By its nature it is a difficult method to measure. Even when the individual firmly believes that the experience has been beneficial this does not necessarily emerge in his relationships with colleagues and others. The evidence to date is scarce and controversial. What is beyond doubt is that capitalising upon emotion and intensity of feeling can be powerful and, therefore, dangerous. As a method, groupwork has gained greatly in popularity. What is urgently needed is more rigorous research into its efficacy.

In chapter 9 Jack Ronaldson provides a detailed account of his interpretation of the method.

Principles in method

A prime consideration in examining any method is the success factor and three important basic principles apply to 'good' method in this sense. Good method should be:

Systematic
Effective
Efficient.

Often methods are used which do not meet the above criteria. An example from education is the 'discovery method'. Taken in extreme form this method is suspect in logic and practice. It would seem that in an age when knowledge accumulates at an alarming rate a method which suggests children will discover everything for themselves is open to serious doubt. Rhodes Boyson (1975) mounts a savage attack on the use of the discovery method as the following quotation demonstrates:

> It is a painfully slow method of discovering the law of gravity to take coach loads of children down to Kent at the time of the apple harvest and hope than an apple will drop on the head of each boy and girl!

An important factor which is often overlooked in any discussion and examination of methods is the rigour which should accompany new developments. Obviously methods will change, but they should change as a result of additional knowledge, experience and research. Bowler and Anthony (1978) undertook a rigorous comparison between two methods of teaching: the demonstration method and the discovery method. Although the findings are complex the important conclusion was a significant advantage for the demonstration method.

Method and theory

A major problem for students on courses in education, social work and other caring professions is in seeing the relationship between 'theory' and 'practice'. It is common for students to protest that their training did not equip them for their subsequent practical role.

Unfortunately theory is often construed as speculative thought implying fancifulness and in many cases students will identify with this use. This is frequently epitomised in the saying 'Oh! That's all very well in theory but it doesn't work in practice!' Although this may be the case it is unfortunate that theory is dismissed as being unimportant. The following definition may be helpful:

> Theory is the exposition of the principles, aims and *methods* of particular subjects and activities (McMaster, 1973).

The teacher and social worker are engaged in a series of practical activities, and the practice of education and that of social work do not aim to increase knowledge, *per se*. In each case the aim is to achieve a practical result. It is here that we see a distinction in education and social work from those rigorous sciences such as physics and chemistry. Education and social work are not in themselves pure sciences. If we can view them as a series of practical activities attempting to achieve a practical result then a concept of theory can be linked to practice and, therefore, method.

Method and skill

Terminology is often a difficulty in professional settings and this is especially true in education and social work. There should be no excuse for lack of clarity, however, and an examination of the distinction between the terms method and skill and their relationship with each other is important.

In most professions which are not exact sciences, one will find words defined to suit certain purposes. It is possible, therefore, to consider method and skill as synonyms, as often happens if one is limited to dictionary definitions. In the development of disciplines and substantive knowledge associated with these disciplines, terms often assume a technical and professional significance. If there is no universally agreed definition then the onus is on the writer to specify his terms to dispel ambiguity. This does not mean that the reader need agree but too often disagreement stems from lack of understanding of the use of the term in the text.

Method and skill can be clearly distinguished. Method has a number of principles (see p.2) but it does not imply *personal* qualities. Method, in this sense, does not include the individual. It is inanimate until operated by the individual. We can discuss method without the person. Skill is personified by the execution of some activity or method and this element of performance is central to skill and is usually measurable. A dozen people can employ the same method but their skill in using that method will vary. As soon as one begins to demonstrate a method then skill is involved.

If 'method' has the criteria previously referred to, and is systematic, effective and efficient, then the 'skills' necessary will be easier to identify, isolate and learn. Unfortunately, there is a tendency to imbue method with skill and the distinction becomes blurred. How many times have we heard teachers and social workers state that they have tried this or that method and that 'it doesn't work'? This becomes a much more complicated issue than appears at first sight; the important point being that all too often methods are discarded by the professional because of lack of skill.

Another danger involved in distinguishing between method and skill is that skills appropriate to a certain setting can be isolated and identified. This is one area where education and social work have traditionally failed. Ideally what is required is 'good' method, as previously described, utilised by a skilled practitioner.

A number of writers use 'technique' as a synonym for method and skill. It is not proposed to enter a detailed discussion on the term 'technique' since this may cause confusion. Sufficient to say that in this text 'technique' and 'skill' can be used interchangeably.

One may make certain assumptions about skill and this has been described at length in one of the companion texts *Skills in Social and Educational Caring* (McMaster, 1982).

It is important to note that skill is dependent upon knowledge and that when these three elements, knowledge, method and skill become appropriately related, then we have the true professional (see figure 1.1).

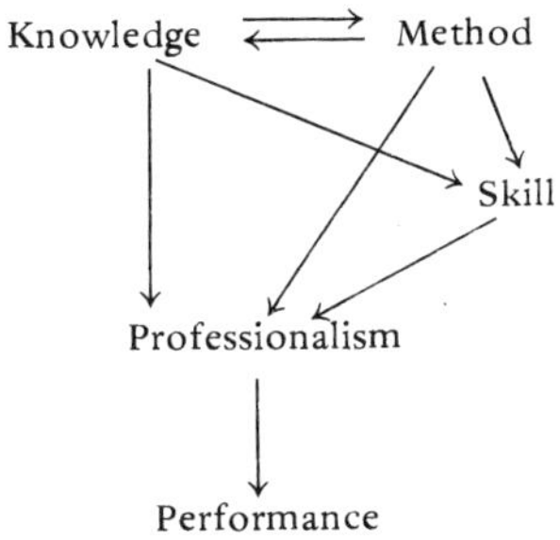

Figure 1.1 The true professional

Method and objective

The relationship between method and objective is critically important. In chapter 2 a brief analysis is given of objectives, but it will be helpful here to highlight some of the major reasons for their importance. Objectives are concerned with specificity and are the antithesis of generalisations and vague statements. They fulfil important functions:

1 They are essential for assessment and evaluation.

2 They offer an articulate means of discussing in detail the content of programmes, syllabuses, documents, courses, and in doing so allow for increased accuracy in communication.

3 They help us determine the most appropriate methods most likely to achieve those objectives.

When objectives are clearly stated but not achieved it gives us the opportunity to examine the reasons for the lack of success and in many cases this may be traced to a method which is inappropriate.

In education and social work there is often a notorious absence of clearly stated objectives with the resultant problem of ill-defined and inappropriate methods.

References

Bowler, L.A. and Anthony, W.S., 'Teaching in Junior School by Demonstration and by Guided Discovery', *Educational Studies*, vol.4, no.2, June 1978.

Boyson, R., *The Crisis in Education*, Woburn Press, 1975.

Jones, Maxwell, 'Towards a Clarification of the Therapeutic Community Concept', *British Journal of Medical Psychology*, vol.32, no.3, 1959.

McMaster, J.McG., *Toward an Educational Theory for the Mentally Handicapped*, Edward Arnold, 1973.

McMaster, J.McG. (ed.), *Skills in Social and Educational Caring*, Gower Publishing Company, 1982.

2 Assessment in concept

JOHN McGREGOR McMASTER

It would seem indisputable that assessment in care and education is important. But assessment means many things to many people and this makes it hard to give a precise, concise and acceptable definition. The following would appear admirable:

> . . . to analyse critically and judge definitively the nature, significance and status of . . . the child (*Websters New International Dictionary*).

Under scrutiny such a definition presents a number of difficulties. What do we mean by 'analyse critically'? What do we mean by 'judge definitively'? What do 'nature', 'significance', 'status' really mean?

If answers to these more obvious questions were readily available, a further problem, probably of greater dimension, would involve the question *How?* Thus, even if we could explain what judging the nature of the child was all about, this does not tell us how to do it. 'What' questions and 'how' questions are important in the analysis of assessment which will be discussed later in the chapter.

Perhaps an easier starting point is to consider assessment as a form of measurement. Parents, teachers, social workers, psychologists, psychiatrists and a host of other groups are interested in the progress or the deterioration of the child. If such factors or progress can be measured then it will be possible to produce evidence to support and substantiate generalised statements suitable for all interested professionals. The accuracy of the measurement will be crucial.

There is a number of aspects of measurement which, when applied to the human, can be clear and unambiguous. For example, height and weight can be measured. These measurements become quantified and may be recorded for the purposes of comparison which allow definitive statements to be made about progress or deterioration. The 12-year-old child who steadily loses 3lbs each week gives rise for concern. Apart from noticing a change in appearance the facts are there and unequivocal proof exists to show that on 1 July 1979 the child weighed 8 stone 10lbs and on the 22 July 1979 the child weighed 8 stone 1lb.

Much of this measurement approach manifests itself in many types of tests, and assessment today is often thought of in these terms. One need only look at the catalogue of the National Foundation for Educational Research to appreciate the proliferation of tests, scales and schedules which can be applied to the human being as an aid to assessment. A few examples will illustrate this point.

English progress tests. This is a series of 14 separate tests designed to provide a continuous assessment of English skills from 7 to 14 years. Each test may be used to give some indication of the progress a pupil has made in aspects such as vocabulary, comprehension, grammatical construction and written expression.

Basic mathematics tests. A series of five tests covering an age range from 7 to 14½ years. The intention is to test some concepts fundamental to mathematical progress.

Reading tests. Five tests which span the age range 6¾ to 15½ years. The aim is to obtain a picture of the child's ability to cope with reading tasks.

The above tests result in a standardised score which makes it possible to compare a child's performance with that of other children of the same age and the child's own earlier or later score.

This would seem extremely helpful, and in many cases it is, provided that educational attainment is appropriate to the problem. Suppose, however, that the problem is 'socially isolate' behaviour (an example of which is given in chapter 5, p.66). It is doubtful if such scores would be especially helpful in assessing the child's isolation.

A popular form of assessment is that of the intelligence test (really a scale), as exemplified by the Terman Merrill revision of the Stanford Binet, or the Wechsler Intelligence Scale for Children. These scales result in the notorious I.Q. What they give is an estimate of general intellectual ability which allows comparison of one child with another, or with an established norm. In other words it is possible to see if a child is above or below average. Although such scales are extremely useful for certain purposes, taken by themselves they are relatively unhelpful and sometimes dangerous, as for example in the indiscriminate labelling of children as 'mentally handicapped'. Other ways of measuring behaviour are available and again we must ask the important question – is the assessment being undertaken appropriate?

The answer is to be partially found, at least, in a statement of aims and the specification of objectives. The distinction between these terms, aims and objectives, is seldom thoroughly appreciated and testimony to this point is often their use as synonyms. Since accurate assessment is an impossibility unless objectives are stated with precision the need for an understanding of this distinction is paramount. Suppose we take the classic aim reiterated time and time again in education, social work and other related spheres: 'to develop the child to the maximum of his intellectual, social, emotional and physical potential'. Left in isolation, as it all too frequently is, it becomes meaningless. What is intellectual potential? Social potential? Emotional? Physical? These cannot be assessed unless specified objectives are supplied. Of course, it is much easier to be general than specific. Specificity involves much work and in many areas of human behaviour it is extremely difficult to articulate objectives. Difficulty is no excuse for not attempting the exercise.

It may be helpful to pursue this relationship between aims and objectives since appropriate assessment procedures are so dependent upon it. Consider an aim as a general declaration of intent. Such a declaration will give an indication of the broad area under consideration.

An external examiner asked to assess students would experience difficulty if simply given a general aim for the course such as, 'to study at an advanced level the conceptual and operational elements of care and education'. Much more information is required if there is to be reasonable assessment with any degree of objectivity. Otherwise, he is faced with making entirely subjective assessments on 'advanced level' and 'conceptual and operational elements'. Supplied with the following objectives derived from the general aim, the picture changes.

Students who complete the course successfully will be expected to:

1 Provide written evidence of knowledge and understanding of current literature in care and education.

2 Demonstrate ability to apply this knowledge and understanding in discussion in both written and verbal forms.

3 Distinguish between broad aims and specific objectives in social work and education.

4 Develop a systematic series of objectives linked to the rationale for a selected establishment.

5 Display at an advanced level the following skills:

   explaining
   questioning
   reinforcement
   reflection of feeling.

6 Design an investigation which has relevance for care or education; collect and analyse data and present these in the form of a dissertation.

7 Analyse specialist treatment programmes for problem children.

8 Design individual treatment programmes for children with behavioural difficulties.

9 Take a focal role in co-ordinating reports from psychologists, psychiatrists, teachers, social workers and other relevant personnel and making responsible decisions.

10 Plan and implement an appropriate in-service staff training programme.

11 Complete satisfactorily a planned individual programme of practice and observation in practical settings.

Evidence can now be looked for to see if these objectives have been reached. This will result in a much more accurate assessment of the students in the context of the objectives supplied.

With individual children the problem is similar. For example, the teacher may have the general aim 'to teach John to read'. He is unable to assess this as it stands with any degree of accuracy, for reading is possible at many different levels. Five 'look and say' words would qualify, as would reading the editorial page in *The Guardian*. For the purposes of accurate assessment it becomes the responsibility of the professional concerned to follow up general statements of intent – the aims – with specified objectives derived from the aims.

Aim – To teach John to read.

Objectives – To introduce the following words: house, shop, church, boy, girl, baby, dog, cow, horse.
– To spend 20 minutes each day with John.
– To attain correct recognition of these words within one week.

When these objectives are made explicit then it becomes possible to assess accurately John's reading ability.

It must be pointed out that the use of specific objectives in the context of assessment is usually more important when there is some problem. Thus with the majority of normal children there will not be the same need to make individual assessment on a specific objective basis. The examples of Ann and Brian in the previous chapter highlight the need for accurate methods of assessment if there is to be progress in the total caring of the children.

Unfortunately, most social workers and teachers err on the side of generalisation rather than specificity. Obviously, certain areas of human behaviour lend themselves more readily to the specification of objectives than others. It follows that such areas will be relatively easy to assess. The more difficult and complex areas of human behaviour make it not only difficult to articulate precise objectives, but also to find the means or methods by which to assess. This state of affairs often results in a quasi-form of assessment in that inappropriate but readily available tests are used to compile information and data. Unless these data are useful, however, such assessment is a waste of valuable time and resources. Even where substantial evidence exists in the form of apparent accurate assessment there must be careful interpretation of the test results. One example will suffice to illustrate this point. A child given tests to ascertain numerical ability scored extremely poorly, but the same child was able to work out complicated bets placed with the local bookmaker. The lesson to be learned from this is that often what appears to be assessed is not necessarily the case. The child in question was able to accomplish with ease the processes of addition, subtraction, multiplication and division, but only in a context which was meaningful to him.

It would seem clear that there is a definite need for information about children, especially when at school. Many teachers believe that knowledge of the child's interests, abilities and personal characteristics is essential for successful teaching. In 1976 at Ruskin College, James Callaghan (then Prime Minister) stressed the importance of teachers assessing pupils in order that they could monitor progress and assess the effectiveness of their teaching. The survey by HMIs (Schools Council, 1978) explained the importance of assessment and transfer records and the Warnock Report (1978) makes a strong plea for careful recording, especially in the light of supporting advisory staff and other professional groups.

The Warnock report emphasised the importance of assessment in a number of ways. All information considered relevant educationally should be shared between professionals, notably teachers and social workers. This information should also be shared between parents and professionals. It is recommended that schools maintain two files on each child, one containing a record of progress and factual information which would be readily available to parents and children. The second file should be confidential with various professionals' assessments and information given in confidence concerning, for example, social background and family relationships.

Warnock recommends five stages in the assessment of children, the first three being school-based but stages four and five involving a multi-professional assessment team. These latter stages would be carefully documented and once a child had been assessed his progress would be reviewed every year by the local education authority's special education advisory and support service.

Although Warnock was set up to review provision for handicapped children, many of the recommendations are of a preventative nature and applicable to all children. This makes it a most important government report for all professionals involved in the total care of children and young people. With one in five children requiring 'special education' in some form, the need for a sound method of assessment in social and educational care becomes critically important. Currently there is a lack of systematic structure in education, social work and the health services. This point was more than adequately stressed by the Court Report (1976), which called for a multi-disciplinary approach by professional staff with greater willingness to work together. The Court Report recommended special district assessment teams for children with staff from health, education and social services. The basic staff would include:

community paediatrician
nursing officer
specialist social worker
principal psychologist
specialist teacher
administrative staff.

This multi-professional approach to the total care of the child recommended in Court and Warnock is not yet operational. Unfortunately, as

Rogers (1980) points out, it is often professional opposition from the professional associations which is the stumbling block. Although this inter-disciplinary integration is desirable in the method of assessment, it is also vital in a social and educational caring approach to the total child.

Parents in the main are most concerned about the progress or lack of progress by their children in school, and rightly so. This suggests the need for some form of accurate recording of information. Too often we have the stereotype of the traditional report card with classic phrases such as 'could do better', 'lazy', 'needs to concentrate more', 'tries hard'. These are virtually meaningless to the parent who wants much more detailed information. Detailed information which is helpful is vital.

> Teachers have expectations – cognitive, physical and social – as well as parents. They need to know what has gone before and what degree of mastery has been achieved. Schools should be places where breadth of personal competence is an aim: informal schools can offer a range of experience and that is all right, providing the teacher can put the stress on competence. It is too easy otherwise for children to flit rapidly from one activity to another without picking up anything more than a superficial gloss (Schools Council, 1978).

There is little standardisation about record keeping. These three examples show very different approaches:

> *Jane*
>
> 'I remember when Jane, asked to spell 'microscopic', wrote 'mincropert'. This must have been several weeks ago. Today I wrote 'mincropert' on the blackboard, and to my great surprise she recognised it. On a diagnostic spelling test she spelled 'tariff' as 'tearerfif'. Today she wrote 'tearfit'. What does she do in these cases? She closes her eyes and makes a dash for it'.

This is the personal log type of record – immediate, vivid and lively.

David

Test scores	At 6 yrs	At 7 yrs	At 8 yrs	At 9 yrs	At 10 yrs
Reading	138	125	125	128	140
Spelling	135	121	120	104	124
Study skills	117	123	129	109	116
English	126	131	121	118	123
Mathematics	130	129	128	126	134

Average score = 100

This is a collection of standardised scores which give some hard information but nothing on the child as a personality.

Jason

Science subjects	*Marked*	*Average*	*Limited*
Interest		√	
Power of observation		√	
Use of source material			√
Ability to read and interest		√	
Development of concepts			√

This is a typical school record card – quick to complete, but extremely limited.

Assessment in the form of record keeping seems meagre and the variability of format in local authorities is considerable. For example, in one authority's primary schools, the six years recorded information on the child appears on a card measuring ten inches by eight. In another, the progress report in mathematics for each year is contained in a space the size of a postage stamp.

A somewhat different system emerges in another authority where the assessment of speech is either 'well enunciated', 'reasonable' or 'defective' – no other answers are acceptable. In another, language is assessed as 'adequate', 'limited', 'severe handicap' or 'no English'. It would seem that this authority does not believe that there are any children with more than 'adequate' language. What of this example in recording the attitude of parents to their children? – 'Neglectful', 'Normal' or 'Over-protective'. Or this one of the child's character?

Character:	Court appearances
	Probation
	Behaviour and reliability
	Industry

Areas of human behaviour which are difficult to assess accurately concern emotion and feeling. Most readers will be acquainted with the normal distribution curve much referred to in, say, the distribution of intelligence throughout the population. One wonders about the real problems confronting us in everyday behaviour. What of the distribution of frustration throughout the population? How does one assess humour? What of fear, anxiety, anger, depression, apathy, aggression, curiosity, kindness and sadness? And there are many others. These would seem to be the elements which often constitute, in some way, our behaviour pattern. Yet, we know that they can change dramatically in time and in a variety of contexts. How do we assess these? Can they be assessed? Is it possible to come anywhere near the definition given at the beginning of the chapter: 'to analyse critically and judge definitively, the nature, significance and status of the child'?

In chapter 3 Denis O'Connor examines this problem of assessing the emotions. Some answers to these points may be found by looking at those special establishments set up as observation and assessment centres for children who enter care.

Observation and assessment centres

A brief historical background will help in understanding the place and, perhaps, function of these centres. A recent milestone was the Children and Young Persons Act (1969). Section 36(4) was of especial importance:

> Every regional plan shall contain proposals for the provision of facilities for the observation of the physical and mental condition of children in the care of relevant authorities and for the assessment of the most suitable accommodation and treatment for those children.

Earlier in the chapter it was mentioned that the need for individual assessment would be more necessary when there was some problem and children who enter care present society with a problem.

Subsumed under the label observation and assessment centre were the old remand homes and reception centres, plus the formal classifying schools which became regional assessment centres. The aims of these observation and assessment centres are stated in part of Section 36 quoted above: '. . . facilities for the observation of the physical and mental condition . . . and assessment of the most suitable accommodation and treatment . . . '. But there would appear to be a considerable discrepancy between observation and assessment centres in practice. The following description of four centres puts this in perspective.

Observation and assessment centre A

This was a classifying school before the 1969 Act and admits boys of 10 to 16 years of age. They come from a wide geographical area, often well beyond the new regional boundaries. The majority are disturbed boys likely to need a lengthy period of residential care. A waiting list of 100 boys is not uncommon and the centre can accommodate 52 boys at any one time. There are two houses, one for boys of 15 years and over, and one for boys aged 10 to 14 years. Each house has a certain autonomy and is staffed by a team leader, nine teachers/housemasters and two housemothers. Approximately half the child care staff have some form of qualification. The overall responsibility for both houses rests with the headmaster and, in his absence, the deputy headmaster. The centre has, on a full-time basis, three educational psychologists and a social worker. The services of two consultant psychiatrists are available. Six full-time secretaries are employed.

Boys normally spend six weeks at the centre and a case conference is held, usually during the fourth week. The conference is chaired by a senior member of staff. In attendance is the boy's field social worker, one or more of the educational psychologists and as many of the house staff as are available. Recommendations are made at this meeting concerning the most appropriate residential establishment in the light of the assessment presented. What, then constitutes this assessment? A typical report runs to some ten typewritten pages and contains the following information:

A summary of relevant factual data, e.g. date of birth, address, father, mother, siblings.

A report on the home background prepared by a member of staff based on reports received from the field social worker.

A list of significant events in the boy's life, e.g. schools attended, court appearances, family difficulties.

A description of the boy's characteristics, e.g. relationship to members of staff, other boys. (This is an impressionistic report by members of the house in which the boy resides.)

A report by the educational psychologist which includes the results of a WISC, comments on personality, and other factors considered relevant. These are the result of two interview sessions with the boy.

A report by the psychiatrist based on a ten-minute interview and a reading of the boy's file.

A report by the school doctor including general state of health and any specific defects, e.g. sight, hearing.

An educational report based on information from tests and other work undertaken in a two-day period during the second week of the boy's stay. A group of 8 to 10 boys is formed from boys admitted the previous week and the teacher who takes the group for the two days writes the report of some 250 words. This is divided into three sections: English, mathematics, and attitude and behaviour.

Standardised tests are given: Burt Spelling Test
Schonell Silent Reading Test R4B
Staffordshire Arithmetic Test
One NFER English Progress Test
One NFER Maths Attainment Test.

Each boy writes two short essays from a choice of titles, one factual and one fictional, and produces a short project on a topic of his own choice.

The report is written as soon as the two-day period is completed.

Observation and assessment centre B

This centre accepts children from the area of the controlling local authority. It accommodates a maximum of 32 boys within the age range 10 to 17 years. The main function of the centre, according to the headmaster, is to select an appropriate placement for the children, having due regard to their needs, background and abilities. The staff comprise a headmaster, deputy headmaster, third-in-charge, one full-time teacher and five child care staff. At the time of writing there was a vacancy for a further full-time teacher and also five full-time child care staff. (The problem of recruiting suitably qualified staff is common in many observation and assessment centres.)

The average length of stay for a child is 10 weeks but this is frequently exceeded and can be as long as 12 months.

The assessment is presented and discussed at a case conference eight weeks after a child has been admitted. This is chaired by one of four people appointed by the Director of Social Services. The headmaster or his deputy attends all case conferences but never takes the chair in his own centre. (He does act as chairman at other centres in the region.) As many staff from the centre as possible attend and the boy's field social worker is present, sometimes with a senior social worker. The headmaster of the day school which the child formerly attended is often asked if the child's class teacher may be present at the meeting.

The assessment report is a pen portrait written by the headmaster under the following sub-headings:

Behaviour on admission
Quantity and quality of personal relationships
Behaviour as an individual
Behaviour with peers
Behaviour with staff
Behaviour with own family
Behaviour with other adults
Sleep pattern and eating habits
Attitude to education
Reaction to outings
Reaction to controls
Absconding, theft and cruelty
Leisure activities

In addition, the social worker's report on the home background is presented together with a psychologist's report and a psychiatrist's report. These latter are obtained as a result of the child's visit to the child guidance clinic but the psychologist and psychiatrist rarely attend the conference.

An educational report is prepared and presented by the teacher. This is based on performance in the classroom together with the following standardised tests:

Burt Spelling Test
Schonell Silent Reading Tests R3 and R4
NFER Non-Verbal Test DH
Raven's Progressive Matrices
Staffordshire Arithmetic Test
Holborn Reading Scale.

The teacher adds a diagnostic comment to the scores and recommends the educational programme he considers most appropriate. The report ends with general comments on the boy's attitude and behaviour in the schoolroom.

A decision is made at the case conference in the light of these reports on whether the child should return home or receive residential care. If the child is still at the centre four weeks later a review meeting is held.

Observation and assessment centre C

This centre can accommodate 30 children, boys and girls, with an age range from 3 years to 16 plus. There are three house units with 10 children in each. The staff is made up of a head, deputy, matron, deputy matron, 10 child care workers, 3 teachers and a classroom assistant. The education unit forms part of the centre.

The average time a child spends in the centre is six months but it is not uncommon for this to extend to two years. Occasionally children will attend the local day school while residing in the centre and a few of the older children have jobs in local factories and shops.

A case conference is held six weeks after the child is admitted. The head chairs the meeting. In attendance are representatives from the Social Services Department responsible for the child, the matron, deputy matron, three care staff and at least one teacher. The consultant psychiatrist and the senior educational psychologist from the local child guidance clinic also attend. A case conference lasts 45 minutes before a decision is made about the placement of the child.

The assessment report consists of:

The social enquiry report submitted by the social worker.

A report from the consultant psychiatrist.

A report listing 'significant events' in the child's life which is compiled by the centre staff.

A classroom report by the teachers in the form of impressions of the child's attitude and responses to the teacher and peers.

The educational psychologist's report with a major emphasis upon the child's background, personality and intellectual functioning.

The houseparents' report on the behaviour of the child within the house unit. This takes the form of a short statement under each of the following headings:

Personal characteristics
Mealtimes (behaviour)
Bedtime (behaviour)
Attitude to other children
Attitude to parents
Attitude to staff
Conclusions.

Observation and assessment centre D

This centre admits boys and girls from 2 to 16 years of age. The staff is comprised of the superintendent, matron, deputy superintendent, senior housemother, four housemothers and two housefathers. There is one full-time teacher and two part-time teachers. Education is provided in two classrooms within the centre.

Case conferences are usually held six weeks after a child has been admitted and are chaired by the principal assistant to the Social Services Department. A typical example of those in attendance is: principal assistant (casework), principal assistant (residential care), social worker, area educational psychologist, consultant psychiatrist and staff from the centre as available. These meetings are held every two weeks.

The final assessment report includes:

The superintendent's summary of the case conference.

Factual information on the child and his family.

A composite report by staff of approximately 500 words under the headings:

Intellectual ability
Medical
Personal characteristics
Interests of the child
Child's relationship with peers
Child's relationship with adults
Child's attitude to and contact with family
Summary of child's present situation.

Report by psychiatrist.

Social worker's report.

Educational psychologist's report. This includes a WISC, a personality questionnaire, and the following educational attainment tests:

Burt's Word Reading Test
Holborn Reading Test
Jackson's Phonic Skills Test
Staffordshire Arithmetic Test
Vernon's Arithmetic Test.

(This centre does not include a teacher's report.)

It can be seen from these descriptions that there are considerable differences in the assessment process. Although all are involved in making a recommendation about where the child should be placed, this presupposes that the assessment carried out should in some way relate to the further treatment, education, therapy or whatever term may be used. If this is logical then it also suggests that the assessment should be concerned with identifying what problems the child has. A closer look at the procedures involved in the four centres raises many doubts about the validity of the reasoning. There is much variation in the length of stay at these centres and it is also disconcerting to examine the constituent parts of the assessment. Can a consultant psychiatrist's report have much to offer when it is based on a ten-minute interview with the child? Are short impressionistic statements by members of staff about whole areas of behaviour a realistic criterion? Is there an over-reliance upon standardised educational attainment tests when the problem may be elsewhere? And anyway, are there realistic criteria for the selection of the tests used? What of information from the child's previous school?

The situation would seem far from satisfactory and many of the difficulties exist because of an absence of clearly stated objectives derived from reasonable aims. The proliferation of observation and assessment centres has proceeded without an adequately articulated rationale. The head of a large observation and assessment centre stated in 1974:

> It is almost an anachronism that Stamford House exists. The whole philosophy of the 1969 Act and child care over the last ten to fifteen years has emphasised the need for individual treatment. How can we do this when we are dealing with 1,043 boys in six months? (Kenny, 1974).

The separation of assessment from treatment is an artificial division which derives largely from the medical model. But the medical model is inappropriate for the assessment and treatment of behaviour problems which are usually anti-social. Perhaps our resources should be geared to changing these anti-social responses into pro-social ones rather than perpetuating centres which are unclear in their objectives and inappropriate in concept. Until effective assessment and treatment become inextricably linked, the prognosis for children is poor. The chapter on behaviour modification (chapter 4) shows that observation, assessment and treatment can be integral parts of a total process.

This view does not seem to be shared by politicians and administrators among whom conflict and defensive attitudes prevail. At central government level there is little communication or integration between the Department of Education and Science and the Department of Health and Social Security. This is reflected in the uneasy relationships between local Departments of Education and Departments of Social Services. It is sad, but understandable, that the professionals in care and education are also involved. Traditionally, psychiatrists are sceptical of psychologists, teachers of social workers, field social workers of residential social workers. These problems have long been recognised and are made abundantly clear in the Court Report (1976) and the Warnock Report (1978).

It is tragic that the casualities are children in need of social and educational care. With this state of affairs currently operating, an integrated approach to the assessment and treatment of children in care is a myth. But it need not remain so. If it were appreciated that the all-important issue is how the child *behaves* in a number of very different environments and harness our resources to *changing* that behaviour if it is considered inappropriate, then much would be accomplished. Most of the environments where professional assessment is carried out are entirely unreal to the child. Interviews with the psychologist, the psychiatrist, the doctor; the time spent with the social worker, the teacher, the residential social worker, are equally meaningless. In the end, behaviour takes place in the neighbourhood environment and what we need are accurate measures of *that* behaviour. If the child is considered violent we need to know when, in what circumstances, how often, who was involved, how long it continued, how he was behaving immediately before and after the violence. This assessment must come from his behaviour in his local habitat.

Certainly other information may be helpful but the problem must be tackled realistically. A simple example encapsulates what so often masquerades as effective professional assessment. A teacher was having considerable difficulty with Andrew who would frequently physically attack other children. This took the form of punching and kicking using extreme force. Occasionally, similar behaviour was exhibited against the teacher concerned and other teachers. The educational psychologist was asked to help and after a number of sessions involving tests, he explained to the teacher that a certain profile indicated that Andrew was hostile to adults. He had, so to speak, proved it! As the psychologist crossed the school yard towards his car, the boy started throwing stones at him and his car. A few minutes later there was a commotion in the corridor and the staffroom door burst open as a dishevelled psychologist struggled to hold Andrew. He finally managed to throw Andrew in the direction of the teacher panting furiously, 'You'll have to do something about this child!'.

Similar examples abound, and until assessment and treatment are seen to be concerned with *real* problems by all professionals involved, the masquerade will continue.

References

Callaghan, James, Address at Ruskin College Oxford, 1976.

Court Report, *Fit for the Future*, HMSO, Cmnd 6684, two volumes, 1976.

Kenny, A., Personal communication, 1974.

Rogers, R., *Crowther to Warnock*, Heinemann Educational Books, 1980.

Schools Council, *Record Keeping in Primary Schools*, HMSO, 1978.

Termann, L.M. and Merrill, M.A., *Stanford-Binet Intelligence Scale*, Houghton Mifflin, Boston, 1960.

Warnock, *Special Educational Needs*, HMSO, 1978.

Websters, *New International Dictionary*, G. Bell and Sons.

Wechsler, D., *Wechsler Intelligence Scale for Children*, Psychological Corporation, New York, 1949.

3 Assessment in practice

DENIS J. O'CONNOR

This chapter complements the previous one by examining assessment from the subjective point of view, that is it gives consideration to the methods by which people are constantly assessing each other whether it is for personal or professional reasons. In this latter respect it describes and evaluates some of the ways in which social workers and teachers need to assess people to care for them effectively.

Methods of assessment, which are ordinarily employed within the caring professions, seem to vary in their effectiveness, as indicated by feedback from those receiving the care. The criticisms which are levelled against the application of objective techniques of assessment in the social services and education can be summarised and expressed in the following way:

> The more objective and clinical the methods of assessing are the more the individual person tends to experience negative feelings and doubts about the effectiveness of the care.
>
> The more subjective and emotionally orientated the methods of assessment are the more the individual person tends to experience positive feelings and hope regarding the effectiveness of the care.
>
> It appears to follow from this that methods of assessment and outcomes from caring are closely linked for the person concerned.

Social workers are often 'adopted' as family by clients who then project on to them the role of helpful 'relative' who must spare no effort on their behalf, which includes spending extra time and professional expertise on their problems. It is inevitable by virtue of the close relationship involved that those who are cared for will expect those who care for them to show personal as well as professional interest in their welfare. For both social workers and teachers the effectiveness of their professionalism can be assessed by the degree to which individuals are helped at the personal level. Further to this social workers and teachers are frequently made aware of how important the pupil's and client's feelings towards the relationship built between them is to the outcome of the care given and therefore how important it is to be liked and trusted by those for whom one cares.

It is as if there is a conspiracy to ignore subjective methods of assessment which operate between people at both the personal and professional level in everyday living situations, and to pretend that no such methods exist and therefore conclude that feelings cannot be assessed. But most people are, under normal circumstances, able to say with accuracy how they feel at any given moment; that is, we learn through personal experience to assess our feelings. Further to this we can build upon the sensitivities we have developed towards our own feelings and through them begin to assess the feelings of others through the methods of sympathising and empathising with the person or group. It seems that the quality and intensity of the others' feelings are unmistakably transmitted to us and in the process evoke traces of similar feelings that we have experienced personally. We can in all honesty say to the person: 'I know how you are feeling'.

In a straightforward way the method of assessing personal problems is to relate as closely as possible to the person or group. The assessment of the emotions necessitates a close encounter with personal feelings.

Reference to an educational setting will make this clear. The teacher assesses the problems his class of 15-year-olds will have with the subjects which he teaches so that he can organise his teaching to help the pupils learn as easily as possible from one stage to the next. The method of assessment which he employs will involve an analysis both of the subject matter to be taught and the ability range of the pupils in the class. The outcome will be determined by intellectual considerations dependent upon an objective approach. But pupils are human beings, not to be programmed by mechanistic methods alone. Such methods, though logically based, give results which are incomplete because they disregard the influence of the emotions upon learning. It is important to consider that each pupil is personally charged with feelings about his life which will affect the way in which he responds to lesson material and to individual teachers. To complete his assessment the teacher should also assess the feelings of his pupils and it is at this vital level of working that the teacher will come to share the same professional concern of the social worker for the individual person. To make assessments of this kind it is necessary to pay serious attention to the emotional behaviour of people which occurs interpersonally in the communications of a caring relationship. The assessment of feelings requires a method which is both emotionally oriented and subjectively based. A further important requirement is first-hand contact with the person to be assessed. It requires face-to-face contact with the person in order to read, that is interpret, the feelings which are motivating the person at any time. This is equally important for both teacher and social worker.

A boy of 15 who had been sniffing glue during breaktime began to argue in the corridor of the school with a teacher who was trying to guide him to his class. Another teacher noticed the heightened tone in the boy's voice and the flushed expression on his face. He also observed the clenching and unclenching of the hands and the snarling facial manner which all added up to the possibility of a fit of violence. Having made this assessment he was just in time to intervene and prevent a fight. His calm manner and friendly caring approach saved the boy from committing an assault on a teacher. The teacher was later able to persuade the boy to have professional medical attention for his glue sniffing habits which served to bring the problem out into the open so that other teachers in the school came to know about it and were careful not to antagonise the boy further while he was receiving care for his problem.

The same boy also presents problems for his social worker who tries to maintain an accepting and helpful manner in spite of the boy's continuing delinquency and troubles at home. She is aware that he feels bored and frustrated with his life and that is why he is so committed to the punk group who are his only friends. He doesn't say much to her but she understands that his whole manner of presentation – the weirdly coloured hair fashioned in the style of a cockscomb, the disfiguring tattoos self-inflicted on his hands and arms, the patterns and colour combinations of his clothes and the provoking strutting style of walking – each 'speak' an individual message of aggression and defiance against authority but collectively express a cry for attention and help. This knowledge helps her to relate more closely to the person and to be supportive without adopting a threatening and judgemental attitude. Her suggestions for change are tuned more towards the needs arising from his problems rather than other people's expectations of him and consider above all the feelings which motivate him.

Assessing the emotional state of a young person from the way he looks, stands and speaks is employing non-verbal communication (NVC) or body language.

This assessment using NVC is essential professional equipment for the social worker and teacher. This theme is developed further in McMaster, 1982.

Having examined this approach to methods of assessment it is desirable to clarify the functions of assessment in caring. To care for someone is to serve the person in a way that is benign and helpful. It is an essentially human activity which cannot be duplicated outside a close personal relationship. In this sense it is absurd to talk about caring as if it happens because an institution, school or hospital is geared to provide accommodation, furniture, equipment, food, drink, warmth, washing facilities, medical services and recreational opportunities. These are necessary accoutrements to caring provision but what constitutes caring itself are certain human qualities in combination. They are:

1 Unconditional and non-possessive warmth.

2 Simply expressed sympathy and empathy.

3 Relating sincerely and with genuineness.

It is within the atmosphere engendered by these qualities that assessment within caring is carried out. Since caring needs to be seen to be caring by the person receiving the care it is necessary for assessment procedures to be:

Non-threatening

Non-judgemental

Non-anxiety-provoking.

To assess in this way requires special knowledge and expertise which will leave the person after the assessment feeling prized and worthy. Assessment procedures so often rely on methods which revert to interrogation and leave the person in a very negative state of mind. Assessment in the context of caring is engineered toward helping the person to feel positive about his self and the conditions of his living. The important thing to remember is that someone is in need of care.

A number of questions arise from this which represent items to be assessed in order to start the caring, such as:

1 What kind of personality has this child?

2 What are the most important things that have happened to him in his life?

3 What is his family background?

4 How does he view himself and his life?

5 How do others assess him?

There are many more areas to be assessed but these examples are perhaps sufficient to indicate the kind of assessments which are needed. It can be seen that the answers to these questions constitute assessments which will be appropriate to discovering the needs and wants of the individual rather than fulfilling the requirements of the school or care home or indeed the demands of the staff. A significant start is made by assessing the level a child has reached irrespective of his chronological age or the expectations of the adults who are responsible for him. When teachers and social workers are engaged in assessment they often underestimate apparently peripheral factors which are in fact central.

Peter, who is five years old, recently changed schools because the family moved house. At the new school he felt insecure and frightened because he was the only new boy and didn't know anyone there. Whenever he left his parents to go into school he cried and during the course of the school day he cried whenever he felt strange or threatened. He had the very good fortune to have a teacher who attempted to reach him at his own level which in this case was regression to pre-school babyhood. She assessed him as needing individual loving care and attention and she gave it to him. She picked him up when he cried, she fussed him in the style of a loving mother. She attended carefully and enthusiastically to whatever he said and did. She stroked him verbally whenever the opportunity arose. She helped him on with his boots after hall activities, she fastened his coat for him when it was time to go home and she made him feel so prized a member of her class that he changed again in three weeks to be self-confident and articulate and normal within the standards of his class and school. The teacher's assessment of him resulted in a highly accurate diagnosis of his needs and the caring she gave was entirely appropriate and therefore effective.

Teachers can so often err by assessing a person's needs according to the standards expected of him rather than recognising the stage he is at. This can result in very serious problems when we are faced with an adult-sized hostile adolescent as in this next example.

Sandra is 15 years old and attends a large comprehensive school. She is overweight and has an unkempt appearance. Her performance at school is poor and she tends to make trouble for some of the class teachers whose assessments of her abilities are extremely low. Recently she seriously assaulted a woman teacher and had to appear in court. When a social worker visited the home he was given a very hostile reception by the family including Sandra who refused all offers of help. Following her court appearance where she was placed on probation, she bought some paracetamol tablets and a bottle of cider and attempted to poison herself. She almost succeeded in committing suicide and was only saved by the prompt action of her sister-in-law who summoned an ambulance. On her return to school she presented as sullen, withdrawn and unmanageable. Her case was referred to the educational psychologist who was called to make an assessment of her.

So much criticism of the style and methods of assessment is levelled at school psychologists that this example serves to uphold the potential value of current assessment procedures when the results are used with relevance to a particular case, and the test interview situation is used as a means of relating to the person. In this example the girl was given the Wechsler Belle Vue Intelligence Scale for Children and her performance caused surprise. The psychologist's report reads:

> My early attempts at establishing rapport with Sandra had been met with a complete lack of response but as I proceeded with the sub-tests and began to feed back to her some approval for her performance she looked directly at me for the first time and began to volunteer small items of information about herself and her feelings quite apart from the responses required by the test, e.g. she read a lot in private secrecy due to the attitude of her family.

It further emerged that she loved Thackeray's novels and some of Shakespeare's tragedies but she was careful to say 'not the way those teachers do it'. The test session lasted well into two hours with Sandra responding increasingly well to the psychologist's questions to the point where she was reluctant to end the session and indicated her willingness to talk further. Sandra surprised everyone by scoring above 140 on the WISC, indicating superior intelligence. She wasn't surprised herself, simply overjoyed that she could share her brilliance in a constructive way with someone who appeared to understand. Further enquiries served to establish that Sandra is exceptionally gifted intellectually and the outcome was the offer of a place in a residential school which she and her mother accepted.

Here again the method of assessment was a routine process used by psychologists every day in their formal assessments of children but in this case what made the assessment appropriate and relevant to the individual's needs and problems was that the whole process of assessment was carried through by a professional who was able to apply a method of assessment which was a combination of objective and subjective approaches. Without the subjective method of assessing and caring for the girl's feelings the objective test score might have yielded a result considerably less than was effectively achieved, which would have made the result both unreliable and invalid.

The important lesson to be learned from these two examples is that Peter and Sandra, both in their individual ways, received the message that the assessments made of them had led to a thorough and positive understanding of them as persons and they were left in no doubt about this because it was followed in each case by suitable treatment.

Many students of the social sciences will be able to identify with the following example which shows similar factors operating in a different context.

A second year honours degree student in the social sciences conducted a clinical interview for his course assessment. The interview was assessed by the tutor in charge of the department who viewed the proceedings through a 'one-way window'. The student conducted his interview with a client with vigour and sparkle and at the end of the half hour joined his tutor expecting to be complimented on his clinical expertise. Imagine his dismay when the professor explained to the anxious student why his interview had been a dismal failure:

> In your interview your questions appeared to be much more important to your method of assessing the client than the person's answers. You were so busy hurrying through the list of carefully prepared questions that you didn't have time to listen to the client and to hear and identify the feelings he was trying to communicate to you to help you understand the kind of person he is and what his real problems are. But you overwhelmed him with your intelligent language and, although he still smiled and responded to you to maintain the illusion of rapport, in effect you had lost him as he had given up trying to reach you and simply endured your questions for the remainder of the interview time. What you did was to impress the client with your personality rather than assess his personality with a view to helping him.
>
> In a more positive approach you might have dispensed with your questions and simply talked to your client person to person. Talk about anything which encourages him to talk and let his personality register on you as if you were a 'photographic film'. Put him at ease, remember he is assessing what you can do for him so be relaxed and friendly to give him confidence in you. It will help you later when you start to give him some treatment and care. After the interview sit down and reflect on what you have learned from the person, develop your mental 'film' of the interview in your mind and play it back in your memory. This is your method of assessment. It is at this stage that you will need your paper and pen to write down what you have gathered from your assessment of this person and in view of your assessments how best to care for him.

The above example serves to illustrate the meaning of assessment as method by showing that it is not simply a matter of asking questions and noting the answers. The method is to gather information of a particular kind which is relevant to the purpose of the relationship. If the purpose is to care for the person then the assessment should provide information on how this is to be done. Assessments of this kind involve an appreciation of the person's feelings as they are here and now and how they might be improved for the benefit of the person.

This method is especially useful to social workers who are working with people in real life situations where the problems rarely require objective intellectual analysis alone but where people desperately need emotional support and help. Similarly in schools there are some teachers who are sufficiently skilled in educating children that they do seem to develop their pupils to the maximum of their intellectual, social, emotional and physical potential at that time. But children need this educational guidance and care at each stage of their development and this is where education in schools frequently fails because not all schools give as much attention to educating the whole person as is usually found in first schools where teachers use these skills as a matter of course. It is unfortunate for children that after the first school stage the organisation in the middle school and most certainly at the comprehensive school levels is engineered towards increasing the distance between pupil and teacher by making the relationship more subject-based. One of the outcomes of this is that teachers see pupils' problems as being largely academic and subject-based rather than to do with feelings. Similarly pupils see teachers as representatives of academic disciplines; the maths teacher, the geography mistress, the head of biology, and not as real people who will help them personally. It follows that the assessments which these teachers make about pupils are restricted to assessing performance in the subjects of the curriculum. The exceptions to this rule only serve to reinforce the inadequacy of the education meted out to senior pupils not all of whom can or want to benefit from specialised subject teaching. The exceptions tend to come from areas of the curriculum where personal contact between pupil and teacher is easier, as happens in handicrafts, home economics, physical education and metal and woodwork. The teachers in these areas of the curriculum have greater personal knowledge about individual children and tend to develop as a necessary part of their work more professional skills in relating to adolescent pupils. It is significant that it is often these teachers who seek satisfaction in developing their careers by post-professional training in counselling courses which provide training in caring skills and methods of assessing pupils' emotional problems and needs.

Social workers know how to assess the emotions; it is a matter of daily business for them to examine the way a person presents himself, to diagnose his feelings from the way he speaks and to comfort and support as well as help him to work towards emotionally acceptable solutions for his problems.

A further example will illustrate this point. All teenagers need time to brood on the mysteries of their feelings as they grow with adolescence, only Marcia brooded more than most. Lacking emotional support and understanding from the adults around her, she spent most of her waking hours with her ear 'glued' to a transistor radio playing popular music. It was her way, in common with many teenagers, of seeking a meaning for her jumbled adolescent emotions which in her case were more insecure than most. The saying that the child who steals, steals love, proved especially true in Marcia's case because she was caught shoplifting and this, together with her persistent truancy, resulted in a care order and she was placed in residential care. A social worker attached to her case had some very penetrating comments to make in her report:

> Marcia missed her father terribly. She blames mother for her father's premature death. Mother is fat and promiscuous. Marcia is thin and lonely. She feels no one loves her and is overwrought emotionally. She suffers extra badly each month with period pains made even worse by her unwillingness to identify with herself as a woman since this would involve, at this stage, identifying with mother. She has no-one to love, and if immediate care and attention is not forthcoming she is liable to become another self-poisoning casualty or even suicide.

It is this professionalism of relating at the emotional level that makes for effectiveness in the caring given by social workers, probation officers, educational welfare officers, child cruelty officers, police juvenile squad and drug squad officers, and home and school liaison teachers. It is the professional awareness of the messages received from the person via non-verbal communication which form the basis for official reports. It is a fact that recommendations filed by these authorities with the law courts serve in many cases to save lives. As one harrassed woman social worker from a London borough put it, 'We have to be able to understand NVC because most of our people can't tell you what they're doing half the time, never mind what they are feeling'. This assessment has the superficial appearance of being uncaring and cynical but a more profound analysis will reveal that if she were unable to make such an assessment the social worker would be professionally ineffective.

For staff in institutions which provide residential care and education, methods of assessing individuals and managing highly charged emotional situations may be more a matter of life and death than simply professional survival. For example, in a small community home with education on the premises there are eight units. Each unit has up to 10 older children and teenagers. At night there is one senior member of staff in charge backed up by a small number of care staff consisting mostly of inexperienced men and women who are learning the job. At approximately 2 a.m. the senior member of staff on duty is awakened by a near hysterical member of the care staff and a group of frightened youngsters who tell a story of assault and stabbing in one of the units. The person in charge assesses the situation in a way that is expressed in the following candid statement:

> If I show the alarm I am feeling, if I run down to the unit and express great anxiety then I can only make matters worse than they are. I must appear calm and reassuring to those present so that they will quieten down and set an example which will serve to de-fuse this potentially explosive situation. Although I want to hasten down there and find out what is happening I will take my time knowing that whoever started this is possibly waiting for my presence in order to gain emotional capital from the situation. I walk slowly down to the unit. Inside the corridor I send the noisy group of agitated young people to their rooms and I force my way into a half-heartedly barricaded bedroom to find one girl defiantly brandishing an ordinary bread knife threatening to kill anybody who comes near her. Another girl lying on the floor in the room is weeping and sobbing that she has been stabbed. On examination she has a superficial scratch on one of her arms but is badly frightened. I send her out of the room, close the door and quietly sit down on the edge of the bed and talk to the girl who is causing all the bother and who has backed off into a corner of the room. After a few minutes she realises that her big emotional scene has come to nothing and she collapses in tears. After a while we are all able to go back to bed.

In this incident it was essential that the member of staff in charge did not precipitate a panic. Her assessment of the situation was right, she knew what she was doing to deal with this crisis. She 'read' the emotional behaviour of the people who started the alarm. This is an example of subjective assessment at a high level.

The reason why many assessment procedures in the educational and social services turn out to be in practice so unrealistic is that they tend to exclude the emotions as important areas for consideration in the assessment. This is understandable as the influence of the emotions on behaviour is a gravely neglected area of education and training. Yet it is worth considering that the emotions are the most influential factors in human behaviour because they serve to initiate, sustain and direct our actions. It is the feelings which we experience which lead us to behave in the ways we do. It is significant therefore that not many training programmes exist to enable pupils in schools to learn to manage their feelings.

Consider for a moment the circumstances in which the social worker has to operate and make important practical assessments of people. For example:

The back yard and the back street;

A balcony of high-rise tenement flats;

The kitchen of a council house where a mother is feeding the baby and caring for three other noisy children;

A crowded lunch-time bar at the local working men's club;

The betting shop amid the background noise of racing commentaries.

These examples are not extremes; they are typical of the day-to-day demands placed upon field workers. The ambivalence of these functions is that they are not at all in sympathy with each other. For, while it is recognised that the social worker will need to relate effectively with people to fulfil a caring role, it is expected that the assessments made will exclude personal feelings and will be based upon objective criteria as outlined in the previous chapter on assessment. This equivocalness exposes the falsehood of the principles on which the caring done within the social services and education is founded.

For example, the social worker who that morning was involved in a decision to commit an old widow to care is upset because her assessments of the situation were very much made on the basis of her emotional appreciation of the problems involved and what she felt had to be done in the circumstances. Now she has to write a report in which she needs to categorically state the objective reasons for her decision couched in language which is unemotional in order to please her superiors. She will therefore cite the untidiness and lack of hygiene in the widow's home, the dishes that had not been properly washed, the floor that hadn't been swept, the windows that hadn't been cleaned and the messy state of the old lady herself. She will also need to mention that there were hardly any stocks of food in the house and the last gas bill hadn't been paid. And she will know that throughout the locality there are many homes with similar conditions where old ladies living on their own will muddle through without being committed to care. She cannot objectively state that her feelings when she saw the look in the old lady's eyes, listened to her quavering voice and observed how slowly she moved, were that she had given up and couldn't care adequately for herself any more, in spite of her tearful protestations to the contrary. In other words, in common with her professional interests, she operates chiefly by the feel of what people and situations are like. But these feelings are not always reliable and valid indices of assessment, and so it becomes necessary to contrive a different set of reasons based upon hypothetical forms of assessment which are very different from those carried out in the actual working situation. The real assessment is based upon a method of emotional appreciation; the stated assessment is based upon a theoretical structure which is a denial of what is felt to be true; that is what upsets this social worker.

Another example from education will serve to emphasise the point. The head teacher and some of the teachers in the school are worried because Joyce, 12 years old, has been observed taking food from the school meals refuse bins. She looks badly bruised and has upset some of the other girls by talking about sexual relationships in a frank and perverted way. Because they are so concerned the teachers refer Joyce's case to the local education authority who ask a school psychologist to interview Joyce. The assessments which were made officially about Joyce stated that her intelligence level on the WISC was 80, her reading age 8 years, arithmetic age 7 years, and her social age 9 years. Afterwards the report was filed and a recommendation was made for Joyce to attend remedial classes which seemed to be no solution for her problems. Unfortunately it appears that she will have to commit a crime or have a crime committed against her for any effective caring action to be taken, a peculiarity of the system which frustrates many social workers in carrying out their caring responsibilities. But all the professional staff who know Joyce feel that this girl is seriously at risk and urgently needs to be taken into care. These feelings are based on the professional assessment of qualified and experienced teachers but they are not considered to be legitimate and acceptable reasons for assessment and will tend therefore to be ignored.

The methods of assessment in the social and educational services present a duality of function which is curiously ambivalent. Traditionally the role of the assessor in assessing human behaviour is concerned with the hard measurable facts of the situation whether it be performance in school or predilection to self-injury or suicide. It is fashionable for local government services to attempt to exclude all but the behavioural data which are open to objective measurement, as is the case when teachers are asked to enter numerical assessments on a card to show the ability levels of a particular pupil who may also have a social service record which lists any misdemeanours and family problems but which says little about the person's potential for growth and fulfilment.

This is paradoxical and surprising in view of the fact that the professionalism of both social worker and teacher expressed in relationships with real people, not figures or profiles in a social services or local education department file. The important criteria to be considered in forming and conducting relationships are human qualities like feelings, hopes and attitudes which for the person concerned are more important than the so-called facts about his behaviour.

The duality referred to earlier may be exemplified especially by reference to the different functions of social service personnel at the two levels of administrator and field worker. At the one level the senior social worker is chiefly concerned with reports and with confidential documents, access to which must be jealously guarded. People are seen through a kiosk window or across a desk with the inevitable form or printed list of regulations to dictate the logical course that the interview, and therefore the relationship, must follow. On the other hand, the field worker is faced with a different set of working conditions. Relationships with people are made at the face-to-face level in circumstances which are constantly changing. At this level the social worker is meeting people on their own home ground. The necessary professional assessments of people and the conditions in which they are living arise out of the quality of contact and honesty of communication which the social worker establishes in relating to those for whom he or she is caring. These relationships are based upon close contacts without any intervening inhibiting factors such as a desk in an office or a form to be filled in. The relationship which develops is determined very largely by the psychological factors of how well the people involved can relate and communicate.

Schools are traditionally places for the intellectual development of children. The caring activities of teachers therefore tend to be restricted to the care of the child's intellect. Witness there are very few school curricula which formally give attention to the education of the child's developing emotions. Assessments tend to be made only in the area of intellectual aptitudes and academic performance. Rarely will an entry be found in a school record card which indicates how a pupil assesses himself in relation to schooling and his feelings towards the teachers and the teaching to which he is exposed. Even the appreciation that the teacher has of the emotional aspects of the child's personality from classroom behaviour tends to be ignored or at most given only passing reference in cliché style at the end of a report as:

> Shows willing but needs to make extra effort.
>
> Must concentrate more and try harder.

The message embodied in the above two instances is begging the real question of why the pupil needs to make more effort or why he must concentrate or try harder. The obvious answer is because the boy or girl pupil doesn't feel it is worthwhile or possible to concentrate more or try harder at the kind of things he or she is asked to do at school. But then these feelings are not usually considered to be important enough to enter into the assessments which are made about the young person.

The denial of feelings, which is an outcome it would seem of normal school practice, seems to operate at a very deep level of our awareness and is constantly expressed in the distrust and suspicion people show towards even their own feelings. Yet it appears to be true from our behaviour that the feelings we have about a person determine how we will assess that person and, more fundamentally, how we will behave towards him. In ordinary terms when we look at another person we tend to appraise his behaviour according to what we see and how we feel about what we see. When we begin to relate to the person we begin to open our assessments of him to include an indication of how he feels about himself and his life and how he feels about his relationship with me. Viewed in this way it can be seen that assessment is essentially a subjective phenomenon whatever the objective circumstances may be and is inextricably tied to the feelings we have for people and towards life. It appears to be true to say that whenever an attempt is made to separate the process of assessment from the context of living people it becomes divorced from reality and is no longer relevant to the problems encountered in everyday life.

In this latter sense assessment is presented as a process of evaluating the state of how things are or what is right or what is wrong with the person or subject assessed. There is a strong element of purposeful activity suggested by this operational definition. For assessment is a practical activity which is directed toward some end. It has meaning only in the sense that it has purpose. Within the scope of this book assessment is introduced as an essential method in the practice of care with children and adolescents.

The source of such skill, it would appear, is chiefly a matter of experience and personality. The professional competence of staff lies in developing insights into disturbed behaviour so that problems may be sufficiently well assessed to ensure that an appropriate and effective course of action can be taken. This is the crux of methods of assessment in practice; if it doesn't work it is no good and another way must be worked out.

For teachers and social workers the foregoing is central to the consideration of assessment as method. Other forms exist but they lack the personal touch. Assessment in practice has a twofold function. On the one hand it has the purpose of clarifying objectives and priorities for assessment such as identifying weaknesses and strengths and ensuring that all aspects of a person's life including his feelings are legitimate matter for attention. On the other hand it involves a process of self-appraisal for the person carrying out the assessment as a safeguard against using methods which are obsolete and perfunctory. With this latter purpose in mind the assessor needs to be guided in practice by a consideration of the following questions:

1. Are you looking critically at what you are doing?
2. Why are you doing it?
3. Are you doing it well?
4. Should you be doing something different?

As this chapter implies assessment has a pragmatic function which in this context is directed towards the care and welfare of the young person. Finally any method of dealing with human problems which does not include caring for the individual person will inevitably be unsuccessful and methods of assessment in practice must take this into account.

Reference

McMaster, J.McG. (ed.), *Skills in Social and Educational Caring*, Gower Publishing Company, 1982.

4 Behaviour modification

JOHN McGREGOR McMASTER

Behaviour modification is arguably the best and most powerful method available to teachers and social workers. But in much lecturing and discussion with diverse groups ranging from short courses for untrained staff to masters degree students, it would appear that the principles of behaviour modification tend to be looked upon as not affecting personal behaviour. It is almost as though behaviour modification is considered a method which remains outside our behaviour repertoire and something which can be picked up and used as though we were reaching for a prescription with the choice of deciding whether to take it. Behaviour modification is with each of us, daily, whether we like it or not.

Conditioning

The concept of conditioning is central to behaviour modification. Unfortunately, for many people conditioning is associated with brain washing and making individuals behave in ways which are contrary to their wishes and, therefore, undesirable. But conditioning can be used positively and profitably to enable people to behave more effectively.

There are two main types of conditioning which everyone has experienced. Most people at some time have had their reflexes tested in which some external stimulus is applied to, e.g. the knee and, assuming that our mechanism is intact, something happens – there is a knee-jerk. This kind of conditioning is usually referred to as classical conditioning and although there is a lengthy historical background it is not proposed to spend much time on it.

A second type of conditioning is more important as an approach in behaviour modification. This is referred to as *operant conditioning*: operant simply meaning that as human beings we *operate* upon our environment. When behaviour takes place there will be a consequence of that behaviour and depending upon how that consequence is perceived there will be a greater or lesser likelihood of the behaviour being repeated. Much of this seems complicated but in reality many everyday settings show the simple elements in operation. This is especially so in teaching and social work.

One of the simplest but most effective examples is to consider a conversation in which two people are involved. When one person starts to speak he is operating on his environment (he is speaking). As a result of his speaking there will be some consequence. This consequence can take a number of forms. For example, the recipient may nod and smile at appropriate points which tends to increase the verbal utterances of the first speaker. In short, the consequences of the talking in this instance have suggested that the behaviour can be continued to become more frequent. Approval has been given. Consider, however, a slightly different set of circumstances. The conversation begins; one person starts to speak (operates on his environment) but the immediate consequence of this talking behaviour is that his companion begins shaking his head violently from side to side and frowning furiously. It is probable that the amount of talking on the part of the first person will decrease, sometimes at quite an alarming rate (unless, of course, he is an experienced politician inured to such conditioning). This behaviour may also be described as increased likelihood of hesitancy and silence.

When the teacher smiles at his pupil he is operating on his environment and the consequence is, usually, a smile in return. Similarly with the social worker and the client. It is no accident that this smiling behaviour is repeated.

A very different example shows the considerable power of this form of conditioning in maintaining behaviour patterns easily. Take the 8-year-old girl who, in a room full of adults, operates on her environment by singing a song. The consequences of this behaviour are that she receives considerable praise and smiles from her 'audience'. These are powerful consequences, powerful reinforcers. It is highly probable that this little girl will wish to repeat more frequently the kind of behaviour which gained so much attention and approval. Consequences of behaviour are referred to as being reinforcing, which simply means that they will affect how that behaviour is more or less likely to be repeated next time.

The reader will be able to think of many situations of a similar nature but with some personal connection.

Reinforcement

There are six basic ways in which reinforcement may be used. These may be better understood if a simple example is given. Let us take the child who makes a verbal contribution to the discussion in the classroom. The behaviour in question then, is 'verbal contribution'.

1 Let us suppose that every time this happens the teacher says 'Good!' When a behaviour is reinforced every time it occurs then this is called 'continuous reinforcement'. In this case, therefore, 'verbal contribution' is under continuous reinforcement.

2 Every time the child makes a verbal contribution the teacher ignores the child completely. This is referred to as 'extinction' and means that the behaviour 'verbal contribution' is under extinction. Eventually the child ceases to make 'verbal contribution'.

3 Every third time the child makes a verbal contribution the teacher says 'Good!' When a behaviour is reinforced after a fixed number of responses this is referred to as 'fixed-ratio' reinforcement. The behaviour 'verbal contribution' is on a fixed-ratio schedule. The number of responses is fixed. Note that if the verbal contribution was every 6th time or 10th time or 15th time this would also be fixed-ratio reinforcement. The ratio of responses is fixed.

4 If the teacher says 'Good!' after two 'verbal contributions', then five, then seven, then eight, this is called 'variable-ratio' reinforcement. In variable-ratio reinforcement the ratio of responses is variable. In this example, the behaviour 'verbal contribution' is under a variable-ratio schedule of reinforcement.

5 The child makes a 'verbal contribution' and the teacher says 'Good!'. At three-minute intervals after this the teacher says 'Good!'. This is a 'fixed-interval' schedule of reinforcement. It is important to note here that the behaviour 'verbal contribution' may not be taking place when the reinforcement is made. It is equally important to note that the behaviour which is taking place when the teacher says 'Good!' at three-minute intervals will be reinforced. Fixed-interval schedules are based entirely on time, e.g. every three minutes, every five minutes, every 30 minutes and so on.

6 The child makes a 'verbal contribution' and the teacher says 'Good!'. After two minutes the teacher says 'Good!' then after seven minutes the teacher says 'Good!'. Here, the schedule is based entirely on time but the time is variable. Thus, we have a 'variable interval' schedule of reinforcement. Again, it is important to note that the behaviour 'verbal contribution' may not be happening when reinforcement is given but some behaviour will be occurring and this will be reinforced.

Reinforcement is often referred to as being positive or negative. This is often confusing to the beginner because in each case we are strengthening behaviour. Thus, both positive and negative reinforcement increase or maintain behaviour which immediately follows. In the example given, the teacher said 'Good!' in each case except number 2 when she ignored the behaviour. 'Good!' for most children is positively reinforcing. This means that whatever the child is doing immediately before teacher says 'Good!' will be strengthened. This behaviour will be likely to be repeated. Suppose the teacher's response was 'Nonsense!' instead of 'Good!' This is for most children negatively reinforcing. The behaviour immediately prior to 'Nonsense!' will be strengthened, but in a negative way. Thus, if the child is making a verbal contribution and the teacher says 'Nonsense!' the chances are that the behaviour of not contributing will be increased.

An important point is that reinforcement varies from one person to another. What is positively reinforcing for Billy may not be for Susan. A football match on television may be a strong positive reinforcer for John Smith but not for Ann Jones.

Everyday behaviour is seldom on a specific schedule, such as those mentioned, for any length of time. Behaviour patterns are extremely complicated but one can select and identify 'pieces' of our behaviour and often explain these in terms of schedules of reinforcement.

For example, a job which is paid £5 for every 100 articles produced is an example of a fixed-ratio schedule of reinforcement. The number, 100, is fixed and when this is reached the £5 is gained. The £5 is the reinforcer.

Gambling, in its many forms, is an excellent example of variable-ratio reinforcement. The notorious 'fruit machines' deliver reinforcement in the form of money (or tokens which can be used as money) after an unpredictable number of responses. Sometimes we are reinforced after 10 tries, 25 tries, 100, 3, 7 and so on. This is the most effective schedule once the behaviour is established.

If an important letter is expected and the postman calls at the same time each day, then the behaviour 'walking to door' is on a fixed-interval schedule.

Suppose you telephone a friend and there is no answer. You try again in 5 minutes, there is no answer. Another call is made after 15 minutes but still no reply. You try again after two hours and your friend answers. The behaviour 'telephoning a friend' is on a variable-interval schedule of reinforcement. The reinforcement occurs when the friend answers. It is the reinforcer that maintains the behaviour.

Token economy

Another area in which behaviour modification can be clearly seen to operate is in token economy. Many people express concern over the efficacy of using tokens as a means of modifying behaviour and as part of a realistic educational or therapeutic programme. The term 'token' means something which has little value in itself but can be exchanged for something which does have value. This may be money or goods or something which is desired by the child or adult. For example, the child may exchange the plastic counter (token) which may have been previously earned for some desirable behaviour, for a chocolate bar or five minutes playing in the sand tray. Sometimes the arguments advanced against such 'token economy' are that human beings should not be subjected to a mechanistic system in which the humanisation process is being undervalued. People who take such a view often have a superficial acquaintance with the kind of animal experimentation in which rats and pigeons have learned a series of tricks. And who are we to be considered rats and pigeons!

In everyday behaviour a large part of the economy is based upon token-type systems. For example in the 1970s many people would drive past a number of petrol stations until they came to one which dispensed Green Shield stamps or other equivalent tokens. Indeed it is surprising sometimes the lengths to which people will go in order to accumulate their tokens. Here, tokens in their own right are worthless. It is only when these tokens can be exchanged for something which has value that they begin to have effect.

In other areas of the economy we find that 'coupons' are offered to members of the public if they buy certain brands. These tokens can then be exchanged for some other form of goods which have real and obvious value. If this is pursued into the realm of credit cards we can see just how far a token economy can go. Later it will be seen that individuals and groups can be organised on a 'token economy' basis and that the principles of such a 'token economy' are similar to those which obtain in our everyday lives.

Change

In attempting to bring about change in behaviour, all too often use is not made of the environment in all its facets. Environment is a term which has limited significance for a number of people because they frequently equate it solely with physical surroundings. Environment, however, is concerned with the total situation in which a person finds himself at any one time. Obviously, then, this includes areas which can be considered social. As soon as a social environment is suggested, people are involved. The permutations of the interactions between people are considerable, and thus we can have a dyadic interaction setting (one-to-one) or we can have the interaction in which a person is involved with a group, and of course we can have interaction in which groups are involved with each other. It is important here to appreciate that although these social environments are in operation they are so in a physical setting. When we begin to realise that it is possible to arrange and rearrange both the social and the physical environment then something of the essence of the conditions for behavioural control can be envisaged. The implications for social worker and teacher in this area are wide-ranging.

Many settings have problems of a very different nature but usually there will be priority ones which are easily identified. Thus the problems confronting the teacher in a class with disruptive children will be vastly different from those confronting a social worker dealing with a depressed client; yet behaviour modification can be fruitfully applied in either of these settings. An additional factor is that although specific environments have problems which are pertinent to their own setting it must not be forgotten that the people who make up these populations are individuals and that individuals have different problems which need attention.

Principles

This is an appropriate point to establish some principles of behaviour modification and stages in implementing a programme.

Although the principles of behaviour modification are relatively few, the programmes which can be established can be complex. Reference has already been made to one major area within behaviour modification, that is operant conditioning. For operant conditioning the following six points give a simple but effective set of basic principles:

1 *Realism:* the desired behaviour must be realistic.

2 *Desirable–undesirable:* desirable behaviours ('pieces' of

behaviour we consider to be improvement) should be reinforced — undesirable ones ignored.

3 *Immediacy:* reinforcement should be immediate.

4 *Frequency:* in establishing the behaviour, the reinforcement should be administered on each occasion of the response. As learning progresses reinforcement should be delivered on an intermittent basis.

5 *Small steps:* the desired behaviour should be built up by small 'steps'. This is done by reinforcing successive improvements.

6 *Environment:* the environment of the learner during the initial stages of learning should be held as constant as possible.

These six basic principles can produce the format for a broad programme and if we add to these five systematic stages which allow the programme to be formulated then we become nearer the implementation of a behaviour modification approach. The five systematic stages are as follows:

1 *Observation:* establish measures of the person's present behaviour (and often past behaviour).

2 *Definition:* define the desired behaviour as specifically as possible.

3 *Availability:* determine the available reinforcers.

4 *Decision:* decide on the reinforcers to be used.

5 *Action:* apply according to an explicit plan.

This may be a judicious moment to elaborate on and give examples to illustrate the six principles and also the five stages.

Realism The fact that the desired behaviour must be realistic, although apparently common sense, is most important. For example, one would not set up 'hearing' as desirable behaviour if we were dealing with a congenitally deaf child. Similarly we would not set up behaviour patterns so far removed in time from the present behaviour as to be totally unrealistic. Thus, no matter how intelligent the 18-month-old baby, it would be unrealistic to set up as an objective the child becoming knowledgeable on a text on behaviour modification in six months' time!

A common failing is to be over-ambitious. Thus the beginner learning to swim may want to cover four lengths of the baths on the first day but this would be unrealistic. However, to achieve several strokes in the water without support *may* be a realistic objective which sets the scene for the future behaviour pattern.

To expect an 85-year-old arthritic woman in a home for the elderly to dress herself as quickly as an 18-year-old would be just as unrealistic. However, the 'dressing behaviour' for the older woman may be *quite* realistic if 40 minutes is allowed.

Desirable–undesirable The second general principle concentrates upon the positive features of behaviour. Thus we should focus on behaviour or behaviours which would appear to be desirable and in some way attempt to reward or reinforce these; conversely undesirable behaviour should in some sense be ignored. It must be stressed that this is an oversimplification but, at the same time, an important general principle.

We must also note that what constitutes desirable or undesirable is not always as easy as may initially appear. In many areas of social behaviour it is usually easy to reach agreement but when dealing with specialist problems, difficulties can arise. Such difficulties should be resolved; otherwise inconsistency results.

Immediacy The third principle is essential in establishing new behaviour. The reinforcement or reward must follow immediately or very closely after the behaviour has been emitted. This is a principle which is seldom carried out in practice even though it is often thought to be so. For example, parents often reinforce their children in acts of behaviour long after the behaviour has taken place. This means that much behaviour will have taken place in the meantime and it may mean that the behaviour nearest to the reward will be that which is reinforced and this behaviour may well be inappropriate.

Frequency When new behaviour is being learned the reinforcement or reward should be given on each occasion that the response is seen to take place. For example, suppose the short-term objective was for an enuretic child to have a 'dry' bed. Each morning that this was the case, the child would be reinforced, until the pattern of behaviour had been clearly established. As this behaviour was maintained the reinforcement would not be delivered every time but on an intermittent basis.

Small steps The 'small steps' principle is a central requirement to effective programmes being introduced. So often when failure has been encountered in learning situations the blame has been placed on the learner when, usually, the person functioning as 'teacher' has been at fault in not arranging the environment in such a way that the steps have been small enough.

Environment A principle desirable in the early stages of learning is to keep the environment of that learner as stable and constant as possible. This reduces 'competition' from other sources and allows for a much better chance of 'success'. In many ways, residential establishments and schools are at an advantage in this respect since the environment can be made reasonably constant. Obviously, it is hoped that later there will be a transfer of the behaviour pattern to other environments and indeed it will be seen that this constitutes a considerable difficulty when more complex behaviour changes are attempted.

Observation Establishing some detailed information about a person's behaviour pattern entails a degree of skill involving perception, observation and recording which is not always to be found in teachers, social workers, parents and others. Perhaps it would be more accurate to suggest that such skill needs to be developed with attention to aspects of behaviour which frequently go unnoticed. It is not feasible to undertake the description of behaviour in all its facets in every context, but it is usually easy to decide which behaviour and which contexts are more important than others. This kind of recorded information is referred to as the baseline measure of behaviour and there are a host of different ways of recording it, some extremely complicated, others very simple. Examples are given in the next chapter.

Definition The second stage may appear straightforward but the specifying of objectives in behaviour patterns can cause great difficulty. A common fault is that the desired behaviour is much too far off and it is unrealistic at that time. Skill is necessary in being able to decide and articulate appropriate objectives. The specification of objectives is frequently thought to have been achieved by some people who believe that they are operating behaviour modification programmes. Under examination one finds that there is much generalisation and if this is the case then it becomes impossible to assess with any degree of accuracy whether the objectives have been met or not.

'To reduce Johnny's aggressive behaviour' may be an admirable sentiment, but left at that level of generalisation there is little hope for any systematic programme which will result in improvement. The reader should see a strong relationship here to the principles *realism* and *small steps*.

Availability Determining the available reinforcers may seem an easy task but in practice this can prove to be deceptive. Obviously there are a number of reinforcers which operate in our everyday society which have positive reinforcement qualities for the majority. These are often referred to as social reinforcers. For example, attention, head nodding, smiling and a certain amount of eye contact are generally considered to be socially reinforcing for most people. What must be realised is that in many individuals the reinforcers can vary greatly and, therefore, what may be positively reinforcing or rewarding for one person may be the opposite for another.

At this stage, as a result of the baseline measures which have been established, it should be possible to isolate some of the reinforcers which seem to be appropriate, or which seem to work for the individual whose behaviour is under scrutiny. At least, one should be able to draw up a list of reinforcers which *may* be utilised in a behaviour modification programme. Such reinforcers are often established as a result of looking at the behaviour patterns immediately before and after some significant happenings. In the majority of cases in which detailed base line measures have been established it is almost always possible to list a number of available reinforcers. This, of course, does not mean to say that they will be 'right'.

Decision Deciding which reinforcers or rewards are to be used becomes dependent largely upon the behaviour which has been specified as being desirable. It must be realised that defining behavioural objectives may also include aspects of behaviour which are considered undesirable. In short, one can usually put the problem in two ways. Earlier the example was given of the child who was a social isolate as far as other children were concerned. On the one hand we can suggest that the desired objectives are to make the child socially acceptable to other children; on the other hand we can state that we wish to eliminate the isolate behaviour. This highlights an important point which is frequently overlooked. In all behavioural settings interaction is a two-way process.

Once the reinforcers have been established and it has been decided which are to be used, then the final stage can be implemented.

Action Features surrounding this stage are that all aspects of the plan are made absolutely explicit to everyone concerned in the treatment or educational programme. If this is not achieved then the chances of success are reduced. Unfortunately, this explicitness seldom occurs, which leads to inconsistencies in the operation of the programme and often results in failure.

Atypical behaviour

Atypical behaviour is something which concerns all professionals dealing with children. It is not always agreed what constitutes such behaviour. This creates a difficulty in differentiating and distinguishing what is 'atypical' as against 'typical', or 'abnormal' as against 'normal'.

One way in which behaviour modification approaches this problem is to look at concepts such as the frequency and the duration of behaviour in specific environmental settings.

If we begin to look at behaviour in these ways then a different perspective emerges. On many occasions when we say that behaviour is 'abnormal' or 'atypical' what we really mean is that it happens more frequently than we expect, or it happens for a longer period of time. Some examples may help to highlight this.

Susan Suppose we venture inside a small unit for adolescent girls and ask a member of staff about Susan. We are told that Susan is a very anti-social girl with extremely aggressive tendencies who can be quite violent. Stop for a moment to consider what this information really tells us. How well informed are we of Susan's behaviour pattern? Suppose the same girl is looked at according to a behaviour modification approach.

Perhaps one could start with a description of the aggressive behaviour in which Susan indulges. This takes the form of shouting, swearing, screaming and striking other girls. Although this helps us to form a better picture it would be more helpful to know how frequently Susan engaged in such behaviour. Thus, does it occur six times in an evening, once a week, twelve times in a morning? Let us suppose it happens on average twice in an evening. Taking this further, what is the setting in which the behaviour takes place? Is it always with the same girls? The same members of staff? When a certain activity is being undertaken? How does Susan behave immediately prior to the aggressive outburst and immediately after? These are the kind of questions which help thinking along the lines of a behavioural approach and which can lead to a programme being established. To think of shouting, swearing and screaming as isolated 'pieces' of behaviour does not necessarily make them 'abnormal' or 'atypical'. Much depends on 'how often' and in which setting.

Similarly with the duration of a behavioural act. For example, it is normal behaviour for a child to spend half an hour on a jig-saw. But if this continues for weeks on end then it ceases to be normal. Note carefully that the behaviour 'doing jig-saws' has not changed but the duration has.

Many examples of this method of looking at human behaviour could be listed but lack of space prohibits. It is hoped that the reader can begin to see the implications when this approach is applied to more complex behaviours.

Residential establishments

The range of residential establishments is wide; provision for children extends to residential nurseries, children's homes, observation and assessment centres, community home schools (the ex-approved schools – called List D schools in Scotland), special residential schools and certain hostels. For adults, there are hostels for unmarried mothers, registered lodging houses, probation hostels, prison after-care hostels, hostels for drug addicts and hostels for alcoholics. There are also a number of homes for different forms of handicap, e.g. the physically handicapped, deaf, blind, epileptics, mentally ill and disordered, mentally handicapped and, of course, there is a variety of residential provision for the elderly.

Although there are many variations in the time spent by residents in these establishments, generally speaking it can be stated that they provide 24-hour care and treatment for the residents. This should make them eminently suitable for the method of behaviour modification. (The 24-hour care and treatment concept is similar to that practised by parents with their children – obviously there may be long periods when the 'residents' are not 'at home'.) The aim for most of these establishments is to return their residents to normal society with the hope that the treatment, education or therapy employed within the residential establishment will not be incompatible with the environment 'outside'. Unfortunately this would seem to be a pious hope at present in the light of many factors. These include lack of resources, untrained staff, inadequate professional support structures and not least a reliance by many people upon a superficial psycho-analytic view of 'treatment'.

In the *Home Office Research Bulletin* (1975) there is a chapter on residential treatment and its effectiveness. The following quotation gives food for thought:

> The model of behaviour which this theory[1] gives rise to implies that intervention in the case of delinquency should aim to modify the consequences of behaviour (the re-inforcements) and the stimuli which elicit delinquency rather than, as has been the traditional way, try to bring about changes in the individual's personality or character. The implications of the model for institutional intervention are fundamental for, whilst removal to an institution may

1 Social learning theory.

protect a child temporarily from the environment which elicits and maintains his delinquent behaviour, attempting to change his behaviour in *another* setting does nothing to alter the environmental factors which contribute strongly to its expression. Nor, the argument continues, does this mean that other non-institutional measures (e.g. probation, community service, intermediate treatment) are likely to be more effective than institutional intervention as they too seek to change the individual rather than the environment. Intervention would more appropriately be designed to reduce the opportunities for learning and reinforcing delinquency; to restrict access to settings which previously evoked delinquency; or to teach pre-social responses to compete with the anti-social ones.

The inadequacy of the programmes operated in the majority of residential establishments suggests a dramatic need for change and improvement. This change and improvement could be achieved by the introduction of behaviour modification techniques to residential establishments of all kinds. A behaviour modification approach with human beings should always involve a specific focus on actions and behaviours which can be observed, not a focus on those actions or behaviours which are inferred. This is a fundamental difference between a behavioural approach and a psycho-analytic approach. A second major point is that there should be a detailed articulation of the treatment which is envisaged. In simple terms the majority of behaviour modification programmes aim at decreasing undesirable behaviour and increasing desirable behaviour. Of course, the definitions of what may constitute desirable and undesirable become something which is not contained in behaviour modification as a method.

Systematic procedure

The following 12-step procedure is designed to make possible clear-cut objectives to be pursued by client and social worker.

The approach is interesting in that the authors (Gambrill, Thomas and Carter, 1971) believe it is appropriate for most, if not all, cases in which a social worker would be involved.

Step 1 List of problem areas

Here the objective is to establish the range of presenting problems as they are seen by both client and social worker. If this can be achieved then each is aware, early in the interaction, of problem areas and each can recognise which problems have priority. This provides a common and agreed basis for action. The social worker establishes this by listing the more obvious problems as he sees them. At this stage there is little specificity.

Step 2 Problem selection and contract

The intention here is to reach agreement between social worker and client on which problems need immediate attention. Once this is achieved it is presented to the client, either verbally or in written form, by the social worker. Such an agreement makes for greater efficiency and more likelihood of early client involvement and co-operation in treatment. If the two parties cannot agree on the problems then the next steps are not pursued.

Step 3 Commitment to co-operate

The objective is to obtain the client's agreement to co-operate fully. The social worker explains briefly the remaining steps of the procedure and emphasis is placed on obtaining accurate information from the client during assessment. The social worker also emphasises that the client's co-operation is vital. This includes maintaining regular contact at appointed times. Again, if agreement is not reached, the system is not pursued.

Step 4 Specification of behaviours

Here efforts are made to be precise in describing the behaviour behind client labels. For example, the term 'nervousness' can have very different meanings for different clients and it is necessary to go beyond the labels and attempt to specify which 'bits' of behaviour are controlling the use of these labels by the client. This is achieved by recording examples of the problem behaviour in the interview and reports of the client's behaviour by other people. If possible, the behaviour is observed by the social worker in the natural environment.

Step 5 Baseline of behaviours

An estimate of the frequency, duration or intensity of the problem behaviour before the social worker intervenes is obtained and this is usually in the form of a report by the client. This is referred to as a pre-baseline estimate. The baseline information is obtained from records kept by the client and other people, including the social worker. The period over which baseline information is obtained will vary according to the complexity of the problem behaviour. For example, a baseline on stammering could be arrived at quickly, whereas problem behaviour as a result of drinking might mean several weeks being spent on baseline information. The baseline information provides the social worker with concrete and specific information. It is also essential for assessment purposes. The authors make the point that Steps 4 and 6 may be combined with this step.

Step 6 Identification of probable controlling conditions

Detailed information is obtained on the client's behaviour before, during and after the problem behaviour. For example, if the problem is depression the client is asked to report and record its time, behavioural acts and events that occur before, during and after each period of depression. Clients may present problem behaviours which seem identical but they will almost certainly have different controlling conditions. On the other hand problem behaviours which are very different may have similar controlling conditions.

Step 7 Assessment of environmental resources

Here, the social worker is attempting to gain access to the controlling stimuli in the client's environment. This will help the social worker to effect changes which will reduce or eliminate the problem behaviour or substitute some alternative considered desirable. Resources may be parents, siblings or members of the peer group. The social worker attempts to establish the available reinforcers. This is achieved in a number of ways, for example, by asking the client what he likes to do in his free time. If the social worker can determine what the client does in his free time this often gives an indication of possible reinforcers.

Step 8 Specification of behavioural objectives

If the social worker's intervention is to be effective then he should specify the behavioural objectives for his client. This will also mean the specifying of a series of successive approximations towards the behavioural objectives. The baseline information will have shown the specific responses that occur. The problem behaviour may include responses which are too frequent and this would suggest objectives that call for a reduction or elimination of that behaviour. Desirable behaviour which is not occurring frequently enough will suggest objectives emphasising acquisition, strengthening or maintenance of behaviour.

Step 9 Formulation of a modification plan

The authors at this stage emphasise the importance of the behaviour modification role of the social worker and a major objective in this step is to select this role. Two main roles are defined, direct intervention and instigation. Direct intervention involves the social worker's activity in the immediate situation and is intended to have a direct impact on the client. Direct intervention may be used in the social worker–client interview but is more commonly used in the external environment. For example, the social worker in the client's home may reinforce selected parental behaviours. Instigation consists of the social worker's specific behaviours during the interview which are used to influence the client's behaviour in the natural environment. Instigation may also be used to change environmental conditions which precede and follow behaviour. It usually consists of an instruction to carry out a certain behaviour in a given situation in the external environment. When the social worker is formulating a modification plan he reviews all the previous steps and the information gained, especially that related to the problem.

If the behaviour modification role is instigation then there are certain criteria which, if met, help towards successful implementation of the programme. Thus, the behaviour to be carried out must be present in the person's repertoire; the client must be able to discriminate the behaviour to be carried out; the social worker must have the ability to influence the client.

The authors suggest that direct intervention is preferable to instigation if it is possible. This is because there is direct impact on the controlling conditions in the client's life situation.

Step 10 Implementation of modification plan

The intention is to modify or maintain behaviour related to the behavioural objectives and the contract made with the client. Intervention is restricted to the area of the contracted problem. It is only after assessment has been completed that the social worker intervenes. This enables him to know precisely what the problems are, their seriousness and the feasibility and appropriateness of his intervention.

Step 11 Monitoring outcomes

The objective here is to obtain information on the effectiveness of the social worker's intervention. This is done by using the baseline data (Step 5) and the information on controlling conditions (Step 6) and looking at the client's behaviour now. The social worker looks for changes which have occurred in the problem behaviour. If there has been no change in behaviour after the intervention of the social worker, he will need to return to earlier steps, analyse and redesign the programme.

Step 12 Maintenance of change

If this stage is reached then the behaviour modification programme has been successful. The objective now is to maintain the desired behaviour for which the programme was undertaken in the first place. It may be that maintenance of the behaviour change can be achieved by using relatives, friends and others who have been associated with the client's problem. Such people can be used as reinforcers. If this is not successful a special maintenance plan may need to be worked out.

Gambrill, Thomas and Carter comment:

> Contrary to the authors' own earlier misgivings and those of their colleagues oriented toward more conventional approaches to practice, it has been found that practice activity can be directed to one problem area at a time, even while others must temporarily be set aside, and that instead of feeling constrained or unduly limited, both client and worker derive reinforcement from the focus and structure the procedure affords . . . . Moreover, so far no evidence has been found of any concomitant negative changes that would merit the term 'symptom substitution'.

An example of this approach in action is given in the following chapter.

Although this 12-step procedure has been suggested in a social work context, it can be applied to many settings in which behaviour occurs. It is easy to see the similarity between the 12 steps and the five systematic stages on p.49. It is important to note one difference. In the 12-step procedure, the client's agreement to the programme is required. Behaviour modification programmes are often instituted without the agreement or awareness of the programme by the recipient. This becomes especially important in dealing with many children's problems.

Modelling

Modelling is one of the most important areas within behaviour modification. Although operant conditioning is extremely powerful, it is difficult to explain all behaviour and learning purely in terms of operants. If we only learned according to operant conditioning it could take a very long time to learn and acquire complex patterns of behaviour. Modelling can provide a considerable short cut. This simple definition of modelling is helpful: a change in behaviour as a result of observing another person or persons.

Sometimes other terms are used in the literature for modelling. These include imitation, vicarious learning, vicarious reinforcement, identification, prompting, role play, social facilitation and contagion. The terms model and modelling would seem simple but explicit.

Whatever the term used, the model provides us with information and frequently serves as a kind of prompt. For example, if a child is unsure of which cutlery to use he will frequently look to an adult model for help.

Society is constantly providing us with models, for example, television, films, plays, radio, advertising, books and, of course, our personal circle of friends, relations and acquaintances. Modelling becomes especially important when one realises it can lead to new behaviour and learning.

There are four major effects of exposure to models.

1 The acquisition of new responses. In this category behaviour is learned which has not previously been in our repertoire.

2 The strengthening of inhibiting responses of the observer. Here the responses are in the repertoire but they are kept in check. Exposure to a model can result in even greater inhibition than before.

3 The weakening of inhibiting responses in the observer. The behaviour has already been learned and is kept in check. Exposure to the model can result in this behaviour becoming less inhibited and, therefore, more likely to appear.

4 The bringing out of previously learned or forgotten responses. The behaviour is already there but unavailable. Exposure to a model reinstates it to consciousness and then it becomes available.

Which of these effects takes place will often depend upon the status of the model in the eyes of the observer and whether the subsequent behaviour of the model is reinforced. It is important to note that individual perceptions of a model will vary enormously. This applies to status and also to reinforcement. It has already been noted that what is positively reinforcing for one person may be negatively reinforcing for another. Similarly, when status is considered it becomes an individual matter. Try to list the following 'models' in status terms for *you*: the Rolling Stones; the Berlin Philharmonic Orchestra; Dave Brubeck; Elton John; the Sex Pistols; Yehudi Menuhin. Consider how a 15-year-old from a deprived and disadvantaged background might list them. It could reasonable be predicted that Yehudi Menuhin and the Berlin Philharmonic would not be in the top two. But the Sex Pistols would.

The reader should contemplate the four major effects of models on observers and attempt some personal applications.

Some examples of modelling are given in the following chapter.

Behaviour modification and 'success'

The efficacy of behaviour modification approaches in a wide variety of settings seems beyond dispute. For example, in group work settings many of the results have been more than promising. This is an interesting development and may come as something of a surprise to a number of people who think that behaviour modification only operates in specialised units with individuals.

Snelbecker (1974) highlights some of the specific areas which have been touched upon in recent years utilising behaviour modification approaches. For example, increase of fourth-year pupils' spelling accuracy; changes in relevant speech productivity of an asphasic through verbal conditioning; effects of teacher attention on study behaviour; reduction of test anxiety, production and elimination of disruptive classroom behaviour by systematically varying teacher's behaviour; influencing classroom study behaviour of pre-school children; developing correspondence between non-verbal and verbal behaviour of pre-school children; reduction of stuttering and stammering; establishing use of descriptive adjectives in the speech of disadvantaged pre-school children; behaviour modification of children with learning disabilities using token economy approaches; use of learning principles in reading acquisition; basic interpersonal relations; improving communication using a self-study programme for two persons; application of programmes of instruction principles to classroom learning; programmed materials for mathematics courses; improving executives' administrative procedures; clinical neuroanatomy by programmed instruction.

The foregoing should give some indication of the diversity of areas in which behaviour modification principles may be applied and there is no doubt that there will be increased emphasis upon behaviour modification in the future. It is a systematic, effective and efficient method.

References

Gambrill, E.D., Thomas, E.J. and Carter, R.D., 'Procedure for Socio Behavioural Control in Open Settings' in *Behaviour Modification Procedures*, edited by Thomas, E.J. (1974).

Home Office Research Bulletin, no.2, Autumn 1975.

Snelbecker, G.E., *Learning Theory, Instructional Theory and Psychoeducational Design*, McGraw Hill, 1974.

5 Examples of behaviour modification in action

JOHN McGREGOR McMASTER

In the previous chapter there was a description of the principles underlying behaviour modification as a method. The intention in this chapter is to describe examples of behaviour modification in action.

It is important to emphasise that behaviour modification is with us all the time. Each of us has learned a great deal and much of this learning has taken place as a result of conditioning, reinforcement and modelling. In everyday settings our behaviour becomes very complex and we are often unaware of which 'bits' are being reinforced. It is only when we begin to examine behaviour patterns in a more systematic manner that the behaviour modification becomes clear.

When the professional sets up specific objectives and uses behaviour modification as a method to reach those objectives he is implementing a programme. The examples in this chapter have been selected to illustrate the progression from simple to more complex programmes.

Let us begin with the student who has the objective of studying in his room. To be more specific he wishes to read and understand Jerome Bruner's text *Toward a Theory of Instruction*. Further, he wishes to take notes on the salient features of the text and to utilise this information in a term essay. The objectives would seem clear. A not unusual pattern of behaviour might be as follows:

The student selects the room for study, his study bedroom.

The student sits down at his table, picks up book, opens book and starts to read.

He takes a few notes but after two minutes, he has the thought 'I think I'll have a cup of coffee'.

The student gets up, makes a cup of coffee and returns to the book.

He drinks his coffee, and thinks 'I would like a cigarette'.

He takes out a cigarette and lights it. In smoking the cigarette he leans back in his chair and his thoughts wander.

Her jerks his attention back to the book but in a few moments decides 'I'll put on a record'. The student selects a favourite record and returns to the book.

He listens to the music and is unable to concentrate on the book. The record ends and he gets up to switch off the record player.

He returns to the book.

The telephone rings; it is his friend who asks him to come out for a drink.

The student, after momentary hesitation decides to go. 'I shall do it tomorrow' he says to himself.

Why should this simple example illustrate some of the elements of behaviour modification in action? Let us examine more closely what has happened. First of all, is the desired behaviour realistic? Certainly, the student should be able to study the text.

Is the desired behaviour being reinforced? Here we can clearly see that this is not the case. What is being reinforced is undesirable behaviour, namely, inattention and distraction. Reinforcement is immediate and the reinforcers are readily identified: coffee, cigarette, listening to record, being with friend, drink in pub. An important point is that if this behaviour pattern is maintained, then in the environment, the room, the student is learning inappropriate behaviour which will be more likely to be repeated next time. If the reinforcers, coffee, cigarette and so on were to be used systematically for appropriate or desirable behaviour then the situation alters. For example, suppose the student sets himself 20 minutes reading the text with suitable note taking. When he meets this objective then he reinforces the behaviour with a cup of coffee. Two hours' study, and then a visit to the pub.

Most of our behaviour is learned although much of what we learn in a more structured setting may not be what the professional involved wishes us to learn. Take the following example.

The teacher's behaviour pattern has become very definitely established. Each Monday morning he takes a lesson for 45 minutes on what is referred to as mental arithmetic. He stands at the front of the class, constantly looks round the room and scrutinises each child. He then asks a question, suddenly and urgently. 'If five books cost a pound what would four books cost?' Occasionally there is an even more urgent 'Quick now!' which can preface the question or come after it. Sometimes both occur and it is difficult to separate the words, 'Quicklynow-if three oranges cost twenty five pence what would ten oranges cost quickly-now!' The teacher looks for cues that provide him with information. If a child looks down or averts his eyes in that situation, he does not know the answer. If a hand begins to rise hesitantly the teacher knows the child is not at all sure. If the arm is waved violently from side to side the child is desperately anxious to be called upon. If there is a puzzled frown or a vacant expression on a face then he knows the child is struggling. If a child is gazing out of the window in a trance-like state he is day-dreaming and not paying attention. These are facts so what is the point of the example? The most important part is that the teacher has established a very definite pattern of behaviour; it is entirely predictable what he will do on a Monday morning. The teacher has two aims:

1 that children will learn mental arithmetic; and
2 as many children as possible will respond.

One child who is very observant is also aware of the information, the cues, at the disposal of the teacher, but since this child finds mental arithmetic boring and uninteresting his two major aims are very different from those of the teacher. The first is not to be caught out and the second to beat the system. The child utilises the same information to achieve his aims. When questions are hurled fast and furiously he looks intensely interested and raises his hand in a deliberate and confident manner. Children who do this it has been noticed are seldom called upon! The teacher preens himself that he can 'cover' the entire class and always knows what each child is doing. When the same child hears the odd question that he *can* answer, he looks out of the window as though day-dreaming. Invariably, the teacher will pounce on the child. Feigning surprise and concern the child hesitates for a moment and then answers correctly. The child has learned a great deal, but not what the teacher intended. The child, here, is programming the teacher's behaviour.

It is easy to think that one is running an effective behaviour modification programme but it may be that lack of knowledge and application result in an increase in undesirable behaviour. The following is a good example. A child came home from school and announced that the teacher had 'a new system' working in the classroom. His mother asked what it was and received the reply 'black stars'. She was intrigued to know what these 'black stars' meant. The child explained that at each table in the classroom one child acted as monitor. The monitor's task was to report any 'wrong' behaviour to the teacher. 'Wrong behaviour' referred to undesirable behaviour as defined by teacher, such as throwing things across the room, rocking on two chair legs, not paying attention, talking out of turn etc. Each time a child was 'reported' by a monitor he 'received' a black star from the teacher! This was duly recorded on a chart on the wall for all to see. In other words it would establish who was the 'naughtiest' child in the class. Between the children, of course, it quickly developed into a competition to gain black stars; the more black stars they collected the higher their prestige rating: even the 'good' children tried to collect 'black stars'.

This is an excellent example of a programme working very effectively but against the objectives set up by the teacher. The teacher had increased the likelihood of 'bad' behaviour by the 'awarding' of black stars. Here is a systematic and sophisticated development of the simple but common error which teachers (and others) commit, namely, to give attention only to undesirable behaviour and to ignore desirable behaviour. In the example there was no incentive for good behaviour but plenty for bad! It is interesting to note that the level of these 'undesirable' behaviours rose sharply as soon as the system was introduced. The reader is referred to page 48 where it can be seen that the teacher was *reversing* basic principle 2: Desirable–undesirable.

A token economy may, however, be operated successfully and imaginatively in a normal school, where the objectives are learning objectives. The teacher, in a junior school in this case study, initiated a programme in the form of a simulated society. In the first instance he set up a classroom society on an imaginary uninhabited island in the South Pacific, with himself as 'the ruler' with divine rights. The society operated initially with a 'currency' of 12 large cowrie shells – these were the tokens. The children became thoroughly immersed in the society and soon devised smaller units of 'cowrie' printed by themselves, to allow the more efficient operation of the island economy. The island moved from slavery to capitalism and then to socialism. The project continued for one whole term with all the children involved in the programme and enjoying it. The understanding of economics which the children had achieved was remarkable – embracing the geography (shape, size, climate etc.), history and religion (earlier civilisation now moved on), biology (plant and animal life useful and non-useful to the farmer) and general science (how to make use of resources and construct things which work) of the island, not to mention the mathematics, English and artistic interpretation necessary for the communication of essentials in the classroom. The children also knew how different social structures developed. In this context the teacher was the planner and manipulator of the social environment. Viewed in this light, the responsibility on the real community is enormous.

Another different example shows a more precise and systematic way of looking at a behaviour problem.

A 4½ year-old girl was causing her parents considerable concern regarding her social behaviour pattern. This pattern manifested itself in persistent and extremely obvious isolate behaviour with regard to children of her own age group. The child was of average intelligence and came from a good home background. An interesting aspect of the girl's behaviour pattern was that she interacted freely with adults but would not initiate contact with other children or respond to other children making overtures to her. Even with a relatively simple behavioural problem such as this we can begin to see the need for systematic planning if consistency and, hopefully, success is to be achieved. The major objectives were to have the child become involved in more play situations with other children and to maintain relationships with those children. The setting for the behaviour modification was a nursery school in which there were 16 children of a similar age.

For the reinforcement or 'reward' the social reinforcement of adult attention was used. Adult attention included a teacher going to, talking to, smiling at, touching, offering and/or giving assistance to the child. Similarly, play relationships were defined as interactions between the child and one or more children; looking or smiling towards each other, touching, helping or working with another child on a project or activity.

Some assessment structure, which would help to evaluate change, or lack of it, was necessary and detailed baseline observations were made on the proximity and interaction of the child with adults and of the child with other children. This was recorded graphically and continued for five days to give an indication of the extent of the problem. The reinforcement procedures were then put into operation by the three teachers in the classroom. They gave attention (positive social reinforcement) to the child only when she interacted with other children. Any approximations to social interaction, e.g. standing near another child, playing beside another child, were to be followed by teacher attention. Thus, as soon as there was any interaction with other children she was given direct individual attention by an adult immediately. When she played alone, she was not given attention and when she contacted an adult she was given the minimum of adult attention, unless she was with another child.

This programme was not successful because adult attention when she was with other children drew her away from the situation which it had been hoped to reinforce. The programme was amended so that adult attention was only given to the child as a participant in the group or with another child. For example, the teacher would address the group and then make reference to the child in question. As soon as there was any suggestion of withdrawing from the group, the teacher would turn away to the other children or equipment. This plan extended over six days and there was a marked improvement in how long and how often the child interacted with other children. As she began spending longer periods in continuous interaction with children the adults' reinforcement became intermittent until gradually she was receiving adult attention in what may be considered normal amounts (Ullman and Krasner, 1965).

Table 5.1 shows this example in a systematic format.

Table 5.1
Example of a behaviour modification programme

Aim	To improve the child's social competence with other children.
Objectives	1 To eliminate isolate behaviour (characterised by standing and looking for long periods). 2 To produce play relationships with other children in the form of conversing, looking or smiling toward each other on a project or activity. 3 To maintain this pattern of behaviour.
Plan	The child attends a nursery class in which there are 15 other children. A detailed observation of the child's behaviour pattern in normal play situations to be undertaken for a period of six weeks. As a result of detailed analysis of the behaviour pattern a programme based on operant conditioning principles to be devised.
Method	The method is operant conditioning with adult attention as the positive social reinforcement. Maximum adult attention to be given contingent upon play (as previously described) with another child and minimum adult attention upon isolate behaviour or upon interaction with an adult alone.
Assess	The objectives were not successfully achieved. Therefore, amendments made to the method in that adult attention was given to the child only when she was a participant in the group or with another child.
Re-assess	The objectives successfully achieved.

It is not necessary to be a psychologist in order to plan a behaviour modification programme. In this example a qualified and experienced teacher of several years' standing attended a series of lectures on behaviour modification. After supplementary reading she decided to try a behaviour modification programme with a child in her class.

Mark was inappropriately active and exaggerated in his responses. If touched lightly by another child he would fall to the floor, yelling and claiming injuries only to recover immediately as something else took his interest. Minor demands or conflicts could produce tremendous outbursts of grief, rage or aggression. He showed limited ability to concentrate on the task in hand, being easily distracted by things and people around him. At times, he showed a singularity of purpose in something he had chosen to do and efforts to stop him failed. It was as though he had made up his mind to be difficult.

He was apparently anxious to make friends with other children but he seemed unable to cope with relationships in his peer group. He found it difficult to share his belongings yet wanted those of other children. He was unable to accept losing a game.

The resultant behaviour was kicking, punching and breaking things. This was usually followed by tears. He had verbal outbursts including swearing. Mark was the most advanced in academic attainment in this remedial class in a normal school, although still some way behind the average child of his age, except in reading. He did respond to individual attention and praise though the duration of the response was short-lived. It was impossible to satisfy his demand for attention while working with a large group.

The teacher began to observe Mark's behaviour in greater detail and made notes. The problem behaviours were narrowed down to the following:

1 Calling out and shouting in class.
2 Kicking, punching and hitting other children.
3 Singing, whistling and chanting repetitively.
4 Yelling unexpectedly.
5 Not listening to instructions.
6 Taking other people's belongings.
7 Disturbing other children.

Attention seemed to be the most obvious reinforcer. The teacher was constantly speaking to him, telling him what to do, what not to do, to start or continue his work, persuading, cajoling, threatening, explaining.

Mark was also receiving much attention from the rest of the class. They were highly amused by his antics. He made them laugh, surprised them, provided endless entertainment which the teacher inadvertently took part in. It was realised that the class were by no means passive receivers of this entertainment. They quickly learned how to provoke and encourage Mark to perform for their amusement. They deliberately nudged him or jogged his chair as they passed because they knew he would react with a yell or fall off. They hid his belongings and deliberately swapped toys with him only to want them back later. They teased him and called him names to provoke a reaction.

The priority problem was how to improve Mark's behaviour and work output. At this stage baseline measures were recorded. These included the amount of work Mark had produced over five consecutive maths and English lessons. The teacher then pointed out to Mark that there were a number of activities which he liked but did not have time for because he did not finish his work. He agreed and after discussion he chose these activities:

1 Feeding the gerbil and the mouse.
2 Collecting privet for the stick insects.
3 Playing with plasticine.
4 Painting.
5 Watering the plants.
6 Having an extra turn reading to teacher.

The teacher thought that a variety of activities would be much better since some would be more suitable than others at certain times.

The teacher had established the reinforcers. It was suggested to Mark that a plan should be made whereby he would agree to finish the work he was set and could then choose which activity he wanted. He accepted this with enthusiasm, wrote out the list of activities and stuck this on the inside of his desk lid. The plan began the following day.

Initially the teacher devised shorter units of work with a view to lengthening them as Mark (hopefully) progressed. Figure 5.1 shows the results of the programme which lasted four weeks.

It can be seen from the graphs that Mark's work output increased considerably. The teacher felt that this was largely brought about by the reinforcement of the immediate rewards he selected for himself, but also partly due to the social reinforcer of praise and the feeling of achievement he experienced when a piece of work was completed. Mark's unacceptable behaviour also decreased. Not least important is the fact that this experienced teacher considered that the approach had shown her that behaviour can be observed, isolated and examined systematically in a manner that she had not thought of previously; and that a soundly constructed behaviour modification programme does work.

The classroom is a most suitable environment for the implementation of behaviour modification programmes because structure is already there.

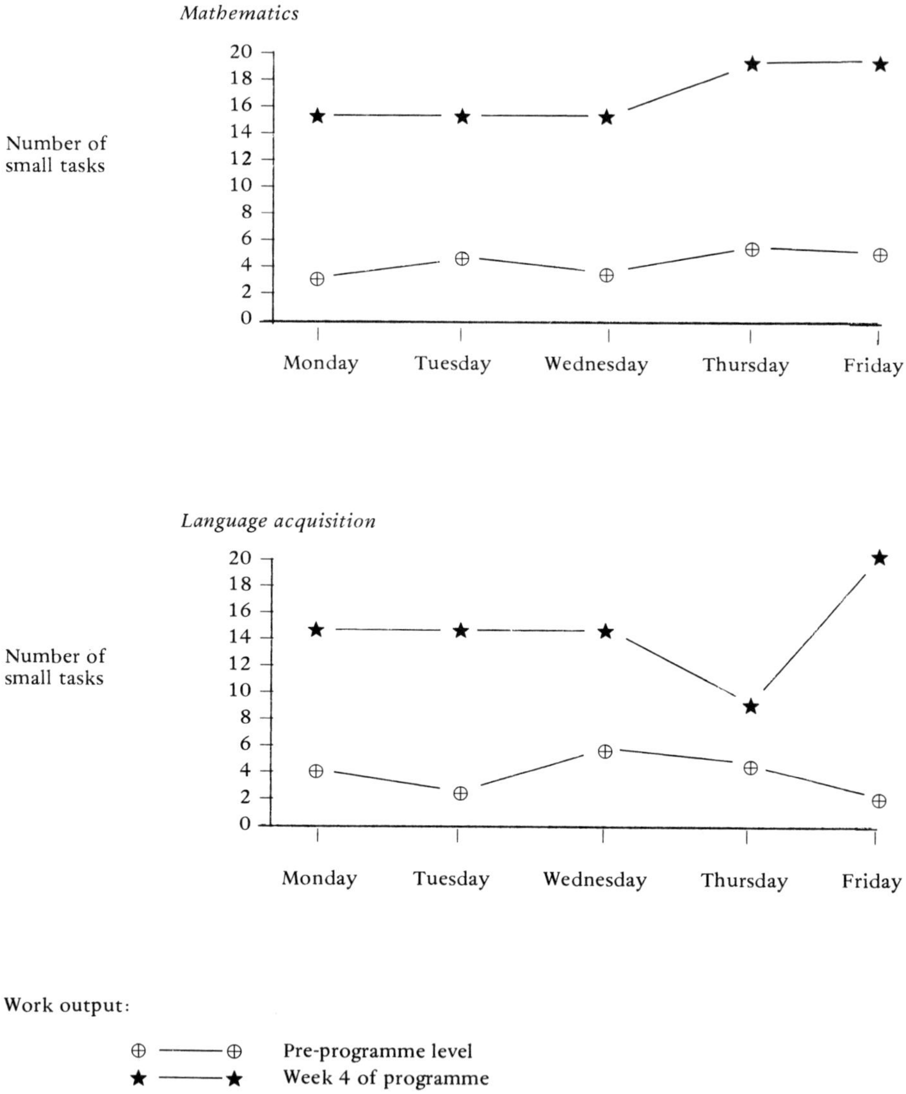

Figure 5.1 Mark's work output

The next study illustrates a simple behaviour modification approach to a common problem in a one-to-one setting which is less formal.

A 13-year-old boy who was the subject of a care order met his social worker for the first time. During the interview the boy made constant reference to how tough he was and his language was punctuated by much swearing. He described many violent incidents in which he claimed to have been involved and made frequent remarks about how he was going to 'get' a number of other boys. There was reason to believe that much of the violence described had not in fact happened. The social worker also knew that the boy was well known in his peer group for constantly boasting about his toughness and violence.

The social worker suspected that the attention the boy received when describing such behaviour was sufficiently reinforcing for him to continue to repeat it. She decided that by listening to him she was also reinforcing this behaviour. The social worker then made a frequency count of the number of references to toughness or violence. This was achieved by 10-minute samples over four interviews. The average number of references to toughness and violence was 10 per minute. This was the baseline as can be seen from figure 5.2. On the sixth interview the social worker decided to ignore any reference to violence.

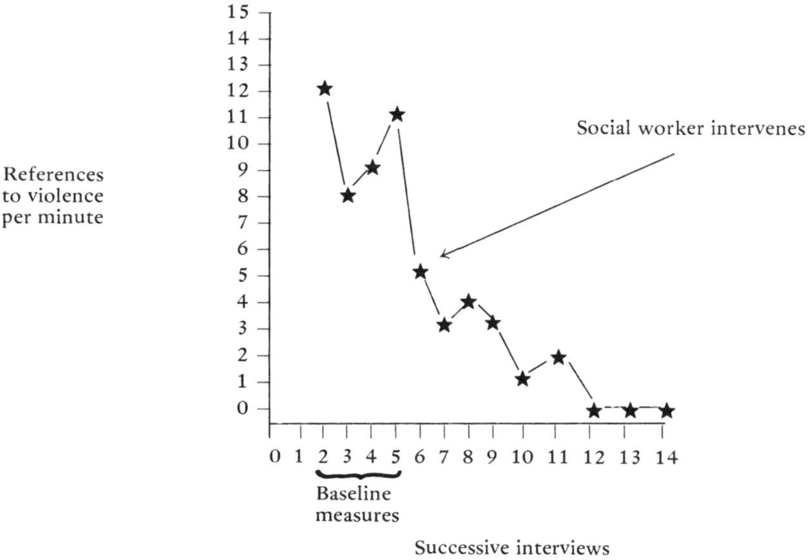

Figure 5.2 References to violence

Ignoring took the form of looking away and then asking questions on the theme of caring for animals. (It was known to the social worker that the boy had been fond of a dog when he was younger.) After five successive interviews each of 30 minutes, the rate of references to violence and toughness had dropped to two per minute. Swearing was also noticeably reduced although this was not specifically monitored. At this point the social worker decided to discuss the problem openly with the boy. He stated that he did not like being 'tough' but was unable to explain why he had kept referring to it. The social worker made a contract with the boy. If he could sustain 'normal' conversation in the next 30-minute interview she would buy him a coca-cola. During the next three interviews there was no reference to toughness or violence.

Behaviour modification is equally effective with older clients as the following example demonstrates. The client was a young married woman who experienced prolonged bouts of depression. It was established by the social worker that when depression was most acute it was accompanied by long periods of crying. Since 'crying' is much more tangible and therefore measureable than 'depression' the objective established was to reduce this crying behaviour which would also reduce the depression. Rather than set up a programme which would reduce undesirable behaviour, an attempt was made to find behaviours which could be increased. If there were times when the woman did not cry then the behaviour at that time could be considered incompatible with crying (and depression). Although the woman was no longer working, the social worker ascertained that when she had been working there was no crying in the work setting. It was also established that certain activities were not associated with crying. These included reading, cleaning the house and shopping.

The woman agreed to the social worker's suggestion that she would take a job. Also it was agreed that a systematic and structured programme of the activities which were considered to be incompatible with crying be instituted early. This would, hopefully, increase behaviour which was not associated with the problem behaviour.

It is interesting to look at the results. From figure 5.3 it can be seen that a pre-baseline measure, estimated for a three-year period, was two to three prolonged bouts of crying per week. The baseline, taken over seven days, shows 10 prolonged bouts of crying.

There are two main elements in the programme: the 'instigation to work' (i.e. the direction from the social worker) and the 'activity programme'. One week after the 'instigation to work' the periods of prolonged crying have dropped to six. The activity programme is introduced and over the next week the crying drops fron six to nil. When maintenance of change (see page 58) becomes effective the non-crying

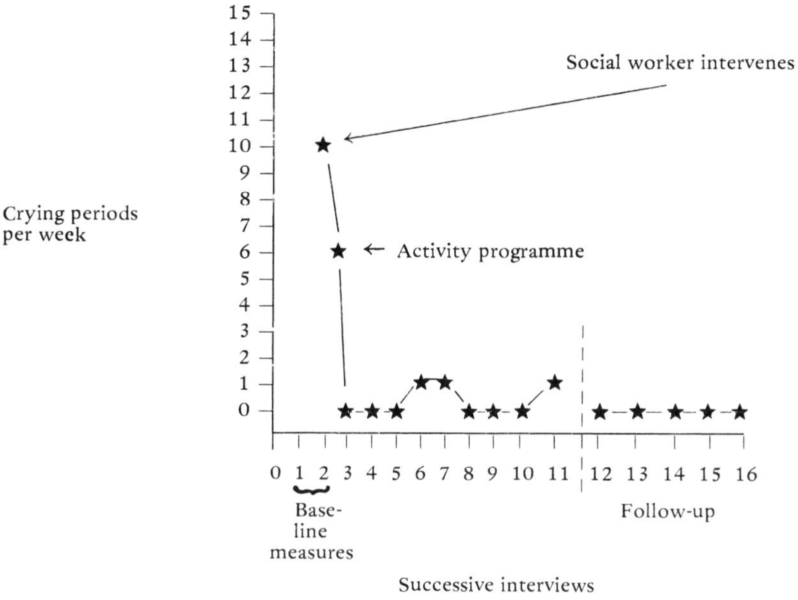

Figure 5.3 Periods of crying

behaviour is established.

After intervention, a five week follow-up based upon the client's report shows less than one per week.

Examples of modelling

In the previous chapter some of the basic characteristics of modelling were explained. We often see simple examples of modelling taking place around us in everyday behaviour.

Parents are the most influential models in the lives of children. This is certainly so in the early stages. Even when the baby is only a few weeks old, it is interesting to watch the interaction between baby and mother. The baby models herself on the mother's lip and mouth movements. When the mother smiles the baby smiles. When the mother puts out her tongue the baby attempts to do the same. This early modelling or imitative behaviour is important for later development. The mother has high status for the baby, who is often receiving reinforcement in the form of food and attention. Much of the early learning is modelled on the mother and we can see the effects in the form of the acquisition of new responses.

A friend was intrigued by the behaviour pattern of his four-year-old daughter. When she was playing by herself she would hunch her shoulders, push her hands down by her sides, walk backwards and forwards with exaggerated long strides and with a pencil in her mouth. The friend, a social worker, mentioned this to his wife who later asked the little girl what she had been doing. It transpired that she was being 'daddy when he's working'. The social worker had not fully appreciated that when he was studying he would often pace up and down, with his hands thrust deep in his pockets, shoulders hunched and puffing intensely on his pipe. His wife was able to confirm this.

If the relationship between child and parents is strong then the parents will have more status. This also means that they will have more influence on the behaviour of their offspring. Sometimes this is not appreciated when, for example, the parents become very concerned about certain behaviours only to realise that they have probably been instrumental in bringing them about. This is seen frequently in smoking and drinking behaviours. The child observes this behaviour from a high status model and reproduces it.

A parent was watching his 10-year-old son Ronald playing with the boy next door. A quarrel ensued and Ronald started punching the other child. The parent became very angry and dashed round to scold Ronald, which he did by shouting at him and shaking him. The parent, unwittingly, was presenting an aggressive model to his son. It is quite feasible that Ronald would learn this behaviour and perform it in the future. Parental influence can be extremely strong, but we do not always realise how this power is being used.

All children go to school and an important influence on their lives is 'teacher'. Next to parents, teachers are often the most significant adults for children, especially in the early years at school. It is an interesting and illuminating experience to see children playing at 'being teacher'. When this happens the child reproduces the behaviour patterns which he has observed in the classroom. Rodney, in spite of a rather unsettled background of shuttling between home and community home, could read well for his six years. He frequently read on his own without prompting. One day the teacher found him in a corner reading to a group of non-readers. It happened to be a favourite story for the class and much to the teacher's amusement he not only read the story but imitated the questions she usually asked at appropriate points in it – with remarkable likeness in intonation – '*What* do you think happened *next*? Where *could* they go now?' Children will often vie with each other to be the teacher in their play settings since the teacher has high status as a model. When we watch the child engaging in this modelling behaviour it can tell us much about the teacher. The child may display responses which would not be considered desirable behaviour by the teacher but which have been learned from her!

The examples used so far have involved 'real' people. There is also considerable evidence which shows the power of films and television as models. A good example can be seen from the varying effects of a film such as *Clockwork Orange*. In this film there are a number of violent scenes, some involving the use of a knife by a young man. A 50-year-old woman interviewed after seeing the film had found these scenes abhorrent and this had clearly strengthened inhibitory responses in this direction. On the other hand a 17-year-old youth stated in court that he had stabbed another youth in the same manner as he had seen in *Clockwork Orange*. He had probably acquired new 'stabbing behaviour' and certainly the effect had been to weaken any inhibitions he may have had.

When television appears to be doing society a service by showing scenes of violence on terraces at football matches, it is probable that there are two major consequences. First, the scenes act as models for other young people and, second, those involved in the televised scenes are positively reinforced by seeing themselves on television.

The effects of modelling were shown in a classic study of aggressive behaviour in young children. One group observed a 'live' adult woman engage in aggressive behaviour towards a life-size doll. The aggressive behaviour included kicking, punching and verbal aggression. A second group of children saw a filmed version of similar behaviour. A third group saw a cartoon filmed version in which the adult was dressed as a clown. A fourth group saw a film in which there was emphasis upon non-aggressive behaviour. A control group of children did not receive any specific modelling. The experimenters observed the behaviour of each group subsequently. The most important findings were that the groups exposed to the aggressive models (real-life, filmed and cartoon) exhibited more aggressive behaviour than the control group and that the group exposed to the non-aggressive model showed less aggressive behaviour than the control group. The groups were matched for age, intelligence and background (Bandura, 1971).

An area which is often conveniently overlooked is that the professional is subject to influence just as much as anyone else. Indeed, in some cases, the 'profession' may suggest models which work against the education or treatment of the child. The professional may fit the behaviour into a system or give it a label so that the education or treatment may become legitimate.

Terms such as 'untestable', 'psychotic', 'disruptive', 'destructive', 'apathetic', 'dangerous', 'slow learner', 'hyperactive', 'above average', can conjure up mental models as a result of the professional's knowledge and experience.

A frightening example of professional influence and the effect of a high status model is shown by Temerlin (1968). Temerlin made a tape recording of a normal man who had excellent relationships with his family and his colleagues. The recording was then played to various groups of mental health professionals who were asked to evaluate the mental health of the man.

The categories open to the group were psychotic, neurotic and mentally healthy.

In the first group there were 20 professionals and immediately prior to the tape being played an outstanding professional remarked loudly to the person next to him that this was an example of a truly normal person. All 20 plunged for mentally healthy, that is, 100 per cent.

There were 24 professionals in the second group and they were informed that the tape was an employment interview. Twenty-nine per cent judged the man neurotic and 71 per cent mentally healthy.

There were 21 professionals in the third group, and there was no suggestion prior to the tape being played. Forty-three per cent classified the man as neurotic and 57 per cent mentally healthy.

The fourth group was made up of 25 psychiatrists. The outstanding professional remarked loudly that this was an example of psychotic behaviour. Sixty per cent put the 'normal' man in the psychotic category and 40 per cent put him in the neurotic category. *Not one of the 25 judged him mentally healthy.*

In the fifth group there were 25 psychologists and a similar suggestion was made. Twenty-eight per cent placed him as psychotic, 60 per cent neurotic and 12 per cent mentally healthy.

In the final group there were 45 graduate students in psychology. The same suggestion was made. Eleven per cent judged him psychotic, 78 per cent neurotic and 11 per cent mentally healthy.

Such an example makes sobering reading and should be compulsory study for all professionals involved in any form of caring.

There is a strong body of research evidence available which shows that models are extremely influential in modifying behaviour, for example, the effect of sharing and helping behaviour (Aderman and Berkowitz, 1970; Bryan and Walbeck, 1970), and the use of models to increase effectiveness in asking questions (Rosenthal, Moore, Dorfman and Nelson, 1971).

These examples show the diversity of the method of behaviour modification in action. Used systematically in the right hands, its potential in effectiveness and efficiency cannot go unheeded.

References

Aderman, D. and Berkowitz, L., 'Observational set, empathy and helping', *Journal of Personality and Social Psychology*, vol.14, 1970.

Bandura, A., *Principles of Behaviour Modification*, Holt, Rinehart and Winston, 1971.

Bryan, J.H. and Walbeck, N.H. 'Preaching and practising generosity: Children's actions and re-actions', *Child Development*, vol.4, 1970.

Rosenthal, T.L., Moore, W.B., Dorfman, H. and Nelson, B., 'Vicarious acquisition of a simple concept with experimenter as model', *Behaviour Research & Therapy*, vol.9, 1971.

Temerlin, M.K., 'Suggestion effects in psychiatric diagnosis', *Journal of Nervous and Mental Disease*, vol.147, 1968.

Ullman, L.P. and Krasner, L., *Case Studies in Behaviour Modification*, Holt, Rinehart and Winston, 1965.

6 Intermediate treatment reviewed

WILLIAM S. MORE

In its short life of 12 years, intermediate treatment is proving to be one of the most difficult concepts in social work and education to define. At one level, it is described cynically as 'treats for delinquents' and as 'something we've been doing for years without the fancy title'. At a more conceptual level, it has been described as:

> a range or combination of programmes and provisions aimed at bridging the gap between the two extremes of compulsory removal of the young person from his family and community, and of leaving the young person in his environment without any controls or treatment provisions (Leissner, Powley and Evans, 1977).

At least this definition tells us clearly what 'intermediate' means, but what about 'treatment'? An anonymous practitioner is responsible for the following explanation:

> Intermediate Treatment is an inter-disciplinary, community-based intervention into the psychological world of the young person in such a way that his individual needs may be met more appropriately, his dysfunctional adjustment to society be stabilised, and his felt conflicts of adolescent ambivalence be resolved (More, 1978a).

Although this definition is hardly in the best interests of public relations, it does clearly imply that some kind of change in the young person's attitudes and behaviour is being sought in the process of intermediate treatment. The central figures involved in this change will be social workers and teachers.

Other definitions add more meaning to the concept. A study group of practioners described intermediate treatment as:

> a method of social work with children which adds new dimensions to supervision, both statutory and voluntary, seeking to improve the quality of life of young people through community-based opportunities for personal growth and development (Social Work Services Development Group, 1977).

That is, intermediate treatment is an aid in the supervision process of social work and education. It has a compensatory function. A final example of the definitions put forward suggests yet another function:

> Intermediate Treatment is action through a range of community-based programmes planned to meet identified needs of children and young persons who are at risk of appearing or have appeared before the Courts (Personal Social Services Council, 1978).

Thus intermediate treatment is not simply concerned with changing the attitudes and behaviour of young offenders, but is also seen as having a preventative function. In this sense as a method it must appeal to many teachers and social workers dealing with children with special needs.

In summary, the evolving definition of intermediate treatment seems to embrace the following:

1. It is a social work interventive strategy aimed at a point somewhere between doing nothing and offering institutional care.
2. It seeks to change delinquent attitudes and behaviour in children and young persons who have appeared before the Courts.
3. It is also concerned with the prevention of children and young people getting into trouble.
4. It is community-based; that is, the prescribed action takes place in the young person's locality.
5. It has a compensatory function, aiming to improve the quality of the young person's experience of his environment.
6. It consists of programmes of activities, specially designed to meet the identified needs of young people.

Additional statements can be made when one looks at what is happening and listens to what is being said. For example, many intermediate treatment projects take place in residential centres many miles from the youngsters' own locality; many have a residential, camping or outward-bound component, and there is an increasing number of day centres often receiving youngsters from up to 20 miles away. Also, many practitioners are now saying that, to be really effective, intermediate treatment must not be social work in its narrow sense, but must be an inter-disciplinary approach to the whole child; for example, the truant may need the concerted contribution of teachers, in providing remedial or compensatory help, of police and magistracy, in making a wisely considered judgement of the youngster's behaviour, of a youth club leader, in creating opportunities for the growth of the youngster's self-esteem through achievement, and of the social worker, in conducting this interventive orchestra.

In the face of all this complexity, it is with a sense of relief and gratitude that we can receive David Thorpe's definition:

> Intermediate Treatment is a generic term covering many projected forms of social work with young people, which, while not purely casework, stop short of full-time care (Thorpe, 1973).

This definition quite clearly reflects the reality of present-day intermediate treatment with its multi-faceted appearance. It also reflects the spirit which has enlivened intermediate treatment from the rather vague Sections 11 and 12 of the Children's and Young Person's Act, 1969, into its kaleidescopic expression today. It was always intended that intermediate treatment should have a 'local' flavour, based on the assumption that what was appropriate in one part of London may not be appropriate in rural Shropshire or in a decaying housing estate in an unemployment blackspot in the North-East. Therefore legislation demanded that the various Children's Regional Planning Committees should develop their own strategies, based on local needs, local interest and local resources. Thus a former Director of Social Work Service (DHSS) could describe the 'official' policy in these terms:

> As a concept, Intermediate Treatment is potentially open-ended and developmental so that it can be sensitive to the rapidly changing social scene rather than be restricted to a static, unresponsive and formalised device used on a tariff system either by Courts or supervisors (Cooper, 1974).

(Although intermediate treatment has undoubtedly developed in an open-ended way, some social workers are reporting their impressions that it is now being treated as part of the tariff system in some Courts;

there is a need however for more objective evidence.)

The policy of open-endedness may have dictated the development of intermediate treatment, yet it has not been without its critics. The DHSS has been accused of lacking imagination in its guidance and of failing to draw up a proper treatment strategy for young people at risk (Harding, 1973). I have argued elsewhere (More, 1978b) that open-endedness is not synonymous with exciting creation; it can just as often mean repeated confusion:

> Therefore, on the one hand there is a richness of local initiative peppered throughout the country; on the other, there is a confused cacophony of developments which often seem to bear no relationship one with another. Many individuals are working hard in an exciting, pioneering way and they claim no little success. At the same time, many mistakes are being made, and repeated again and again because there is little in the way of sharing and learning together.

Even when intermediate treatment schemes were being initiated in the early and mid-1970s, there was still doubt and confusion 'in the minds of the key figures operating the scheme – magistrates, social workers and youth workers – as to the meaning and potential use of the measure . . . the lack of precision in the Act appears to have led some unclear thinking' (Harding, 1973). From the beginning, doubts were expressed about the treatment component for early initiatives gave the impression of being variations on a theme of outward-bound. Should it really be re-named 'intermediate care' (Freeman, 1969) or 'flexible care'? (Prins, 1972). Even today it can be argued that the bulk of what is known as intermediate treatment is diversionary rather than therapeutic in content.

Despite the criticism, an open-ended intermediate treatment has grown out of the legislation and is still with us today. Obviously there must be some reason or evolutionary process at work in this phenomenon, for it runs counter to our human needs for tidiness and clearly defined parameters. In this respect it can hardly be classified as 'good method' as described in chapter 1: systematic, effective and efficient. The exploration of this evolutionary process is the task of the next section. This will lead to a description of the state of intermediate treatment throughout the country, and to a discussion of the dilemmas, pains and possibilities which will dictate its shape tomorrow.

The evolution of intermediate treatment

This is a story which could have a happier ending. It is the story of a triple Odyssey, at the end of which the triumph of homecoming is somewhat marred by the fact that the three Ulysses have each arrived at a different place, and each is as convinced as the other that he is right. The three Ulysses in question are the social welfare services, the educational service and the youth service. We shall follow the journeyings of each in turn as they strove to achieve a relevant service to young people in difficulty, and we shall highlight the particular fears which caused them to panic on the way.

Before 1971, the Home Office was responsible for administering juvenile justice, and also for the welfare of children and young people through its children's department. It is therefore not surprising, particularly in view of psychological and sociological research findings which consistently linked juvenile delinquency with the lack of proper care and nurturing and with disadvantaged and deprived environments, that justice and welfare were to be transformed into care and treatment in the Children and Young Persons' Act, 1963. As early as 1927, the Departmental Committee on the Treatment of Offenders was suggesting that there might be other and more effective ways of responding to juvenile crime than simply locking up the offender. During the postwar years, it was increasingly suspected that many youngsters ended up in Courts because the welfare services were ineffective or perhaps simply inaccessible. The Ingleby Report (Home Office, 1960) recognised that parents often required help in maintaining a stable family life and in the increasingly difficult task of child-rearing. The Children and Young Persons' Act, 1963, reflected these concerns, and gave much wider powers to the children's departments of local authorities in developing preventative strategies. It was this Act which gave birth to family advice centres, whose contribution to the development of intermediate treatment has not been insignificant.

Meanwhile, the Advisory Council on the Treatment of the Offender had been making suggestions in 1962 as to how young offenders could be dealt with non-custodially (Home Office, 1962). Already justice and welfare were moving inevitably closer together. What was happening in practice during the 1960s was highlighting this development. Children's officers were seeing that an early enough 'welfare' intervention might well mean the later avoidance of a 'justice' intervention. Approved schools were becoming more and more open and 'progressive', making many a 'welfare' children's home look like Alcatraz by comparison. Social work theory was ingesting research which suggested that delinquency was a disease caused by bad nurturing and/or bad environment. If it was a disease, therefore it could be cured. The juvenile delinquent does not need control as much as he needs a compensatory nurturing and an enriched environment. But are these not the needs of the 'welfare' children too? Thus the scene was set for the next act.

In 1968, the White Paper *Children in Trouble* was published. The twin strands of non-custodial treatment of the young offender and the non-segregation of the young offender from his non-offending peer were brought together. Offenders and non-offenders should be provided with new experiences and introduced to new interests while still living at home and within their own community. They should be, as far as possible, supervised and supported from their home base. They should be offered a variety of provision and a flexibility of presentation. This was the spirit of the letter made bold in Sections 11–19 of the Children and Young Persons' Act, 1969, although there was no specific mention of the term 'intermediate treatment'. But intermediate treatment had arrived, or at least it would arrive when the children's regional planning committees submitted their proposals. Although that took three years to happen, many projects had already taken root throughout the country, styled as 'intermediate treatment projects'. It was now firmly established, for other reasons which will be elucidated later, as a social work service. Magistrates now had powers to impose a supervision order with the requirement that the child or young person submit himself to a 90 days' or 30 days' process of 'intermediate treatment' (as yet unnamed), but with his permission if he was over the age of 14. The extent to which magistrates have used these powers will be shown later.

It would be quite wrong to assume that the above is a true and fair account of the evolution of intermediate treatment. True I believe it to be, but fair it certainly is not. There were other developments in other fields which were, in their own way, leading to an inevitable conclusion in the concept of intermediate treatment, despite the fact that intermediate treatment was finally defined in a 'social work' Act. (The extent to which this particular fact is simply an accident of history may be evidenced in the difficulty being faced by government agencies in Northern Ireland at present; as the 1969 Act does not apply there, updating legislation is required. The Black Committee, whose task it is to make recommendations concerning new legislation in the child care field, is vigorously rumoured to be unsure about where to place the statutory responsibility for intermediate treatment. It has been strongly argued that the probation service is the most appropriate agency to deal with the management and development of intermediate treatment there.) (More, 1978b.)

The educational services, particularly during the postwar years, were moving increasingly swiftly towards something which looks rather like intermediate treatment. Since 1870 (the year of the Education Act) school attendance officers have been chiefly concerned with children who are absent from school, and parents have been liable for prosecution whether they were aware of their children's non-attendance or not. Out of this basic service, the educational welfare officer has evolved, with a somewhat different and expanded role, due to the recognition that truancy is an effect whose causes may be more effectively dealt with than the effect itself. During the 1960s, research was suggesting quite clearly that truancy could no longer be looked at in isolation from other social factors impinging on the child. For example, truancy was not simply a matter of running away from school; 'it is inextricably tied up with more profound social and educational problems' (Christmas and Binyon, 1970), and there is little difference in background between a group of truants and a group of delinquents (Tennent, 1970). The Seebohm Committee reported (HMSO, 1968) that truancy 'is likely to have much deeper roots and wider implications than the symptom of persistent non-attendance'. In addition, at a very practical level, the educational welfare officer often finds himself, when following up a non-attendance report, as the first agency to open the Pandora's box of a family caught in multiple problems and difficulties. He can refer to appropriate agencies, and he may well judge that his young non-attender is in need of care and protection, perhaps even in moral danger. In this way, the educational welfare officer finds himself in the front line of the social welfare services.

There can be no question that the educational welfare service is about more than school attendance. A bold step was taken in Glasgow in 1945, and repeated in 1950, when welfare officers were attached to some secondary schools. The result was that school attendance rates in these schools increased by a factor of two over the rest of the city. More significantly, while the juvenile delinquency rate was rising throughout Glasgow, Court appearances by pupils in these selected schools dropped by a factor of more than two (Mack, 1956). A similar strategy was employed in a Manchester school in 1966; the attendance rate increased by almost 13 per cent, and during the period of the experiment there were no juvenile Court appearances, although the average number of appearances during that length of period in the past had been in double figures (report from the President of the Educational Welfare Officers' National Association). Thus there was the growing recognition that the educational welfare service was not simply concerned about school attendance; it was inextricably bound up with the prevention of delinquency and with the welfare of the child in the wider context of his family and community.

Meanwhile, within the schools themselves, teachers might well have continued to see themselves as the repository of society's values, and to see parents and the way they live as primary impediments in their task of educating the citizens of tomorrow; yet there were many signs that teachers were seeing their task as bigger and more complex than had traditionally been seen. The Plowden Report (1967) crystallised and formalised a great deal of thinking and activity of a decade in its formulation of 'educational priority areas', the recognition that allowances must be made and compensation offered for the very strong environmental influences on a child's achievement and development. Before this formulation, there had been an accelerated activity by teachers and by schools in a multitude of supporting services. At its least formal, there were school camps and expeditions, after-school 'latch-key' activities and clubs, and evening youth clubs run and staffed by interested teachers. At a semi-formal level, there was the recognition that the teacher had a social caring role, and many of them came to know the homes and the families of their form pupils. At a more formal and organisational level, there was the establishment of remedial classes, which tended to be small and which contained not only the slow learner but also the reluctant learner with a history of either truancy or classroom disruption or both. Specialised units were being established also to which head teachers could refer those pupils whose behaviour was too difficult to be contained within the normal school.

It seems a very small step from that point to the concept of intermediate treatment. I have described elsewhere (More and Jones, 1977) how teachers collaborated over a number of years in a programme of social learning for truants and classroom-disrupters:

> In short, our aims and procedures were not dissimilar to many of the current expressions of intermediate treatment. Within the schools, there is a depth of concern for these youngsters which is continually being eroded . . . . Teachers are in an ideal position for identifying developing conflict and disturbance in adolescents, and they do not have to wait until a youngster has been to court before they know that help is required. The teacher's difficulty is, however, knowing what help is required, and whether he has the skills to offer it.

The educational welfare service and schools were moving slowly but surely to a concept of 'intermediate treatment', just as the social welfare services were during the 1950s and 1960s. The evolutionary processes seem to be moving towards a convergence, but that convergence did not happen because the Children and Young Persons' Act (1969) stepped in to give the formal responsibility for the development of these services to the social welfare agencies, later the social services departments. We shall see to what extent the expected and desired convergence has been achieved in the 12 years since the Act.

There has been, however, a third major evolutionary strand, and that is through the youth service. The Albemarle Report (Report of the Committee on the Youth Service in England and Wales, 1960) had reported that the youth service attracted one in three of the country's youth, and that a 10-year programme of development was required to fulfil the potential of the service. It saw that young adolescents were in a particularly vulnerable position in contemporary Britain; they were confronted with a society of conflicting voices and standards; they were becoming the object of too much attention; their idealism was producing a suspicion of the socialisation process as 'brainwashing'. Following that report, there was a heavy investment of funds from central and local government, and training for youth leaders was developed and expanded. At the same time, the 'detached' youth worker was moving out towards those who would not come to the youth clubs. What was he attempting to do?

> He attempts to establish relationships with young delinquents or children 'at risk' in the places where they usually congregate, but this specialised work is part of a range of services which includes adventure playgrounds, weekend camping and sports programmes, arts centres, community-based playgroups, discotheques and youth clubs . . . [Its] principles of acceptance, flexibility and permissiveness offer opportunities for reaching those youngsters in the neighbourhood who have special problems, such as delinquents, truants or slow learners (Powley, 1974).

During the 1960s, the detached youth worker, using what resources he could find in the neighbourhood, played a significant part in what has been called 'the rediscovery of community work' (Leissner, Powley and Evans, 1977). This recognition of community as resource was so significant as to bring about the change in name from 'youth service' to 'youth and community service'. This was the first recommendation of the Youth Service Development Council (1969).

The developmental strategy recommended for the 1970s contains many features which can be identified with current intermediate treatment. For example, 'those experimental projects which attempted work with young people outside the normal service emphasised the need for flexibility and variety in the service'; an important approach is one 'in which the emphasis is on a relationship which can be established by workers with individuals and groups of young people who need adult help and who will accept it on their own ground'; and again, another approach has an emphasis on 'association between young people, and between young people and adults . . . . Activities flourish and die as required, and the youth workers help young people in relationships, problems and interests inside and outside the building'.

Here again it can be said with some evidence that, if intermediate treatment had not been defined and formalised as a social welfare service in 1969, it would have been invented anyway, this time by the youth service. The evolutionary line of the education service and the youth service during the postwar years seemed set to converge with that of the social welfare service in the formulation of a new service for troubled and wayward youngsters, a service which would have the commitment of professionals from different 'camps'. Somehow Sections 11–19 of the Children and Young Persons' Act (1963) do not encapsulate the fullness or the spirit of that evolutionary process.

There is need for a dual postscript to this section on the background of intermediate treatment. Amongst the earliest pioneers of group work and activity with delinquent youngsters was the probation service. Since 1949, it has been part of the probation officer's duty to encourage a youngster's involvement in youth activities provided in his neighbourhood by both statutory and voluntary agencies. For some, this meant no more than making sure the youngster on probation enrolled in the local youth club. But for many probation officers it meant much more. Many involved themselves in setting up their own evening activities in a probation office, with desks pushed to the side of the room. There were weekend camps and treks, youth hostelling and Saturday clubs, and many 'helping groups' which now appear to have a great deal in common with the community service order. It is possible that the probation service, certainly in some of its more imaginative offices, had actually arrived at, and was operating intermediate treatment before the publishing of the 1969 Act. Young offenders on supervision orders were being offered more than the statutory probation supervision; through an involvement with adults and peers, the offenders were being offered opportunities to learn about themselves, about the world, and about how the two could live at peace with each other.

There was a second rather isolated service busy 'doing its own thing' during the 1960s. The residential service, in particular the approved schools service, was caught up in the backwash of philosophical revolution which had been sweeping through the residential scene from the 1950s. They were now talking about 'treatment', in which 'relationships' were of primary significance. They were beginning to feel guilty when they talked the old language of punishment, containment, control, even social rehabilitation. Staff were sought who 'had something to offer the children', through which 'a relationship could be made'. Into residential care came people with hobbies, interests, and sometimes passions. Approved school management committees were now receiving requests for camping equipment, canoes, ropes and boots for mountaineering, and the occasional Land Rover. This outdoor pursuit-type of activity was not just an important development in residential care, but it also coloured the initial thrust of intermediate treatment in the early 1970s. This development in the residential service before intermediate treatment was established meant that there was a pool of personnel experienced in working closely with groups of youngsters, and perhaps welcoming the opportunity that intermediate treatment afforded them of moving out of the residential service into a more preventative role. It was simply an accident of history that much of the skill and expertise represented in that pool was of the 'outward bound' variety.

There was one movement of the 1960s which is worth mentioning, but should not be over-emphasised. The Duke of Edinburgh Award Scheme was gaining momentum during that decade, and was being invested in by schools, youth clubs and the residential services. It would be wrong to say that this scheme was the genesis of intermediate treatment. It was rather a fairly active expression of certain beliefs and hopes of the time; for example, achievement is important in a young person's experience of growing up; everybody can achieve something, if the choice is wide enough; and youngsters who achieve are less likely to be delinquent. The scheme was something which made sense for many teachers, youth workers and social workers, not simply because it expressed much idealism in a very practical and realistic way, but also because it became a very appropriate tool for that particular point in their evolutionary development. It was right for the times, and the fact that it was there helped the process along.

In summary, intermediate treatment was not created out of a vacuum. Society's evolving beliefs, aspirations and confusions were influencing developments in social welfare, education and the youth service. A growing knowledge of the roots of delinquency and disturbance in young people was expressing itself in a development towards the concept of 'intermediate treatment'. In all the major services concerned with the care and development of children, this evolutionary line appeared to be moving towards an apex, a common meeting-point of development where traditionally separate discrete services would converge and embrace each other. It was at that point that we might have expected to see professional barriers made more flexible to allow for a future development based on co-operation and a pooling of expertise and resources. To what extent has this happened in the development of intermediate treatment and, if it has not happened, what has gone wrong? The next section attempts to answer these questions.

The growth of intermediate treatment

Intermediate treatment received its formal blessing in Sections 11–19 of the Children and Young Persons' Act (1963), and when the DHSS asked the children's regional planning committees to submit their plans. It was to take three years before these plans were finally submitted. However, during that time, there was much activity. Social workers, teachers, youth workers, probation officers and residential child care officers continued to do the kind of things which they had been developing, waiting to see how they would eventually be involved in intermediate treatment. They were looking forward to the stamp of approval, and possibly to the freeing of funds for their various projects. Subsequent events, however, were to take a different twist.

Intermediate treatment became much more ensconced in the new social services departments than anyone expected. They drew up and administered the intermediate treatment budgets, and only exceptionally were schemes included which were outside their control, e.g. in the youth service, probation offices and schools. Voluntary services, many of which were developing programmes with young delinquents and truants in the community, continued to receive funding in the normal way, at the discretion of the social services committee through its 'voluntary organisations' budget, competing with meals on wheels, pre-school playgroups, etc. The result has been that all these agencies who see themselves as part of the intermediate treatment provision have continued to do what they were doing, and to develop their projects independently of mainstream intermediate treatment, by using the new name. Obviously there were exceptions to this trend; a very small number of departments were able to collaborate with other agencies. In the main, however, the situation was, and still is to a great extent, that social service departments established new programmes and posts which attracted applications from social workers, teachers, youth workers and residential care officers. That is, instead of developments based on an inter-agency co-operation, the social services departments invested in an internal development staffed by people attracted from those other interested and experienced agencies. The promise of that apex of inter-agency development has not been fulfilled in the first 12 years of the life of intermediate treatment.

There are two other major influences which have shaped the development of intermediate treatment, and which have conspired to retard that development. First, it has already been noted that the DHSS wished intermediate treatment to evolve in a shape which would be consonant with local needs and resources. This has meant that there has been a lack of specific guidelines and concrete demands. The publications of the DHSS Development Group (1973, 1976, 1977 and 1978) have consisted in the main of description of projects and reports of seminars. Thus the first generation of intermediate treatment specialists found themselves out in the community clutching a job description that did not tell them what to do and where to start. They were pioneers, but they felt more like strangers in a strange land. Supervision and support were sparse; it was a very lonely occupation. Genuine clients were not very thick on the ground, for the magistracy needed some convincing that intermediate treatment had something to offer and would work. So it was that intermediate treatment became an aid in the ordinary supervision process of the social worker; youngsters were referred to the specialist by social workers who hoped that they might respond to the magic of an intermediate treatment programme. But what precisely that programme was and how it should be worked out in practice were the questions for which the specialist was still seeking answers.

There was a second set of circumstances which actually aided the physical growth of intermediate treatment during the 1970s, but which may have had the concomitant effect of holding back a proper analysis of appropriate aims and objectives, methodologies and evaluation. Intermediate treatment was asked to grow at a time when money was becoming an increasingly scarce resource in social services departments, and when local authorities were questioning expenditure on personal and social services. The costs of residential care had escalated since the late 1960s. Intermediate treatment on the other hand could be cheap. It was not difficult to sell it as a cheap alternative to an increasingly expensive institutional care, and as a means of keeping costs down in an over-stretched social services budget.

At the same time as intermediate treatment was growing during the 1970s, the DHSS was also investing heavily in secure accommodation for your delinquents; they were building their own youth treatment centres, and were paying the capital costs of secure units attached to existing residential resources. Also, politicians claimed to be expressing public concerns when they attacked the 'progressives' in society, teachers whose lack of discipline was leading to a lowering of standards, and social workers whose methods were doing no more than providing treats for delinquents. Many engaged in the developing intermediate treatment were confused by the mixed messages they were getting, and it is not surprising that there was a defensive air around much of intermediate treatment.

Obviously the development of intermediate treatment benefited greatly from the cutbacks in local authority expenditure during the early and mid-1970s. It grew magnificently; appointments were made throughout the country. Urban aid applications were successful, and projects were taking off. The committed intermediate treatment specialists were taking advantage of the situation, and many were proceeding to develop very imaginative projects. But the more sensitive were aware of questions which they could not answer. Was all this support coming to intermediate treatment for the wrong reasons? Was its development being aided in order to balance books rather than because of a belief that intermediate treatment is more right for the youngsters involved than is residential care? Was intermediate treatment really just a pawn in a political game played out at a time of financial austerity? Confusions such as these were reported frequently in a national survey of intermediate treatment (More, 1978), and support can be found in research into personality factors significantly present in people working in face-to-face contact with young people (More, 1973).

References

Children and their Primary Schools (Plowden Report), HMSO, 1967.

Christmas, L. and Binyon, M., Times Educational Supplement, no.2854, 30 January 1970, pp. 12-14.

Cooper, J., *Intermediate Treatment*, DHSS, 1974.

DHSS Development Projects, *Intermediate Treatment Project*, 1973; *Intermediate Treatment*, 1976; *Aspects of Supervision and Intermediate Treatment*, 1977; *Intermediate Treatment – Planning for Action*, 1977; *Intermediate Treatment – 28 Choices*, 1977; *I.T. in Action – Film*, 1978.

Freeman, J.W., *Intermediate Treatment in Community Homes and the Approved School System*, Institute of Criminology, Cambridge, 1969.

Harding, J., *Intermediate Treatment*, BASW, 1973.

Home Office, *Report of the Committee on Children and Young Persons* (Ingleby Report), HMSO, 1960.

Home Office, *Non-Residential Treatment of Offenders under Twenty-One*, HMSO, 1962.

Home Office, *Children in Trouble*, HMSO, 1968.

Leissner, A., Powley, T. and Evans, D., *Intermediate Treatment*, National Children's Bureau, 1977.

Mack, J., 'Delinquency and the Changing Social Pattern', Charles Russell Memorial Lecture, 1956.

More, W., 'The Personality of Residential Staff', *Residential Social Work*, February 1973.

More, W., *I.T. – The National Picture?*, PEPAR, 1978a.

More, W., *The National Picture of I.T. in the United Kingdom*, ITU, Northern Ireland, 1978b.

More, W., *Working with School-Rejecting Adolescents 1974-77*, PEPAR, 1978c.

More, W and Jones, J., 'Getting I.T. at School', *Community Care*, 17 August 1977.

Personal Social Services Council, *A Future for Intermediate Treatment*, 1978.

Powley, T., *Youth Social Work*, vol.1, no.3, 1974.

Prins, H., 'An Example of Compulsory Benevolence', *Social Work Today*, 18 March 1972.

Report of the Committee on Local Authority and Allied Personal Social Services (Seebohm Report), HMSO, 1968.

Report from the President of the EWO's National Association, 1968 (EWO's Presidential Report).

Report of the Committee on the Youth Service in England and Wales, (Albemarle Report), HMSO, 1960.

Tennent, C., *Educational Research*, 13 (185-90), 1970.

Thorpe, D., 'Working with Young People', *Social Work Today*, vol.3, no.23, 1973.

Youth Service Development Council, *Youth and Community Work in the 70's*, HMSO, 1969.

7 Intermediate treatment: an investigation

WILLIAM S. MORE

In this chapter a discussion of the results of an investigation into the evolving shape and direction of intermediate treatment conducted in the spring of 1978 is attempted. The official report (More, 1978) concedes a number of difficulties but despite these a picture was presented, based on the exploration of a 20 per cent sample of social service departments in England and Wales.

The consequences of the policy of the decentralised development of intermediate treatment were clearly highlighted. Some areas boasted of well-oiled, sophisticated intermediate treatment machines, while others were just beginning to think about it. Two areas were spending less than £1,000 per annum on intermediate treatment, while another two were spending over £100,000 per annum. Half of the 24 areas in the sample were spending less than £10,000, and the other half were spending between £10,000 and £150,000.

The same variation is seen in the way magistrates throughout the country are using the facility of a supervision order with an intermediate treatment condition. At the time of the investigation, there was one area where no child was on such a supervision order, while another area was producing as many as 29 per 100,000 population. The mean throughout the sample was 10 per 100,000 population. It is suggested that two factors were producing this phenomenon of wide variation. First, what is the point of magistrates making such an order when there are few, if any, facilities for intermediate treatment in a particular area? There was some positive correlation between budget size and number of orders. Second, many magistrates are still to be convinced of the efficacy of intermediate treatment, and similarly social workers are not recommending the facility as they might. This would explain the lack of total positive correlation between budget size and number of orders; one of the highest spending authorities was producing only one order per 100,000 population.

Within the social services departments themselves, only one-quarter were without a full-time intermediate treatment co-ordinator, but for more than half of the sample he (a male in every case) was the only full-time person involved in intermediate treatment in his area. In most areas, there was an admitted reliance on social workers being involved in addition to their normal work, and on volunteers. Only 9 out of the sampled 24 areas had an identifiable intermediate treatment centre with supporting staff, and this varied from thoroughgoing day care, with an educational component, to centres for evening and weekend activities. The wide variation in numbers of social services department personnel engaged in intermediate treatment activities is to be expected where policies are allowed to be formulated at the local level. The numbers of full and part-time personnel involved in such activities varied from only one in one area to 136 in another; the mean figure for the sample was 21.25.

In summary, the investigation highlighted the considerable variation throughout the country in the use and management of intermediate treatment provision; there was no national consistency in the magistracy, nor in social services departmental budgeting and personnel deployment.

In the late 1960s, it was clear that many social agencies were poised to make a contribution to the developing concept of intermediate treatment. To what extent has such promise been fulfilled in the 1970s? Has intermediate treatment developed as an inter-disciplinary approach to children and young people in trouble or at risk? The investigation has produced a picture which once again highlights wide differences from area to area. For example, one-third of the social services departments involve no other agency in their intermediate treatment provision for their areas, while another one-third involve three or more other agencies. The probation service is used by half the departments, while educational welfare officers, teachers, youth workers, policemen and voluntary agencies are each used by around one-quarter of the departments. This information is limited as it gives no indication of the extent of the involvement of these other agencies in intermediate treatment provision. Thus the involvement of a policeman in an evening activity club run by social workers is given the same significance in these figures as a group of educational welfare officers organising their own intermediate treatment programme for school-rejecting pupils. The most which can be claimed for these figures is that they express the involvement in any capacity whatsoever, of other agencies or their personnel in intermediate treatment programmes recognised by social services departments. Of course, in addition to this, most of the other agencies were continuing 'to do their own thing', sometimes calling it intermediate treatment, irrespective of the official attitude or recognition of social services departments.

A more telling detail of the national picture is that of the declared attitudes of social services departments' intermediate treatment personnel towards the other involved agencies. Attitude responses were elicited in relation to each of the probation service, schools and the educational welfare service, the police, and the youth service in terms of their involvement in intermediate treatment. Only 24 per cent of all the responses were positive, while 42.6 per cent were unambiguously negative. (Only one positive response to schools and the educational welfare service was expressed, and half of all the negative responses were aimed there!) Once again, the probation service came out at the top, with most positive responses and least negative. It is not evident from these figures that intermediate treatment is about to realise its inter-disciplinary potential, certainly in the near future.

If intermediate treatment is not being operated by social workers, probation officers, youth workers, teachers, etc., working alongside each other and sharing their respective experience and expertise, who then is doing intermediate treatment as defined in the 1969 Act? Within social services departments in the 24 sampled areas, of all the personnel involved in intermediate treatment programmes, 84 per cent were identified as social workers carrying a normal or slightly reduced case-load. This is not to say that these social workers were doing 84 per cent of all intermediate treatment in their departments, for most of the remaining 16 per cent were full-time intermediate treatment specialists (84 in number). Only five departments did not use their social workers in intermediate treatment programmes, and of these two had little or nothing in the way of intermediate treatment provision anyway.

In summary, following the formalising of the intermediate treatment concept in the 1969 Act, a 'social work' Act, intermediate treatment has been developed statutorily as a service of social workers, despite the fact that there are many agencies with allied concerns and expertise who were ready and willing to participate in its development but who now feel shut out by departmental barriers and negative attitudes. Many of these agencies at local levels are therefore proceeding as if nothing had happened in 1969, producing their own preventative programmes for youngsters, and often calling themselves 'intermediate treatment' for reasons of credibility and public relations.

What precisely are intermediate treatment specialists setting out to do, and what are they providing for youngsters in their programmes? The researchers involved in the investigation reported difficulty in finding answers to such questions. They reported a lack of specificity, even when pressed, in responses to the question: 'What do you hope to have achieved for the youngsters when they leave your programme?' The most common responses were a reduction in delinquent behaviour, the avoidance of residential care, greater skills in communication and relationships, compensation for earlier deprivation, a constructive experience, and the meeting of the needs of the youngsters. As generalised objectives, they are applicable to most aspects of social and educational intervention with children and young people, and are in no way specific to intermediate treatment. Here can be seen the notorious absence of clearly stated objectives referred to in chapter 1 and developed in chapter 2. Interesting to note was the 'single-mindedness' of six respondents, of whom two stated that they were only in the business of meeting the needs of youngsters, and of whom the remaining four claimed to measure success simply in keeping youngsters out of residential care. One is left with the thought that a discussion of objectives was demanding of a little more analysis than that.

When the content of the various intermediate treatment programmes was examined, that is, the ways in which the achievement of these objectives were sought, the researchers again reported difficulty. Of the 24 sampled areas, only 22 had identifiable intermediate treatment programmes in operation. (One was still at the planning stage, while the second was experiencing a hiatus in its development.) All the operating areas were offering 'youth club-type' activities, including table-tennis, pool, darts and football, while the majority were also offering 'outward bound-type' activities, such as camping, canoeing, hiking and mountaineering. Only 10 areas used the vehicle of group discussion of personal problems and behaviour. Remedial education was offered in 6 areas, while another 6 saw 'spending time with individuals' as important enough to mention. Only a small minority of areas offered community service programmes. Further, it was estimated that about 75 per cent of all youngsters involved in intermediate treatment programmes were being offered less than four hours per week, usually in the form of a 'club night'.

Obviously what is not recorded in these figures is the level of personal involvement of those intermediate treatment workers with the youngsters in both indoor and outdoor activities. It can reasonably be suspected that the level of involvement is deeper and more personal than we would normally expect to find in a classroom or in a normal case-work situation, and that it is that kind of involvement and execution of skill which residential workers have found to be notoriously difficult to articulate. So much of their work in face-to-face contact with youngsters is spontaneous and intuitive, and even the most skilled will describe their whole movement towards a youngster as 'natural', rather than as the expression of some learned skill. There is no evidence to suggest that those engaged in intermediate treatment do not indulge in this involvement, but there is certainly the evidence that they cannot talk about it, probably because it is so difficult to identify the elements of skill in it.[1] What can happen in a situation where intuition plays such a large part is that the process is devalued and not seen to have the significance that it undoubtedly has. Also, because one person can do it 'quite naturally', the assumption is that all can do it, and therefore it is not important enough to talk about. Yet many would argue that those intermediate treatment programmes which are apparently effective and successful are not so because of the programme *per se*, but because of what happens within the programme in the interaction of worker and youngster, that is, through the use of these unrecognised skills. The programme is therefore the vehicle of treatment rather than the therapy itself.

I have attempted elsewhere (More, 1974) and in a different context to analyse the process of these 'intuitive skills'. There are four movements in the exercise of interpersonal skills, i.e. concern, sensitivity, imagination and risk. There is growing evidence from the fields of social work and education that the social worker or the teacher cannot even begin to help unless the client or the pupil perceives a concern in the expressed attitudes and behaviour of the would-be helper. This is not simply to do with the words we use; rather it is to do with the total movement and bearing of the helper, coupled with the client's or pupil's previous experience of the helper. The helper moves with sensitivity towards the other person, picking up many cues from the behaviour of the other person, but usually unaware that he is noticing as much as he is. Also beyond awareness, there is a working out process in the mind. The cues are matched with previous experience and learning, and an imaginative jump is made into the world of the other person. Out comes the behaviour, apparently spontaneous, but certainly a risk, for it is usually totally based on guesswork. Sometimes it is right and appropriate, and sometimes it is wrong and alienating; for the more sensitive who are able to hold themselves more open to learning from the pain and success of experience, it is more often right and appropriate.

I am suggesting that people who are 'good with youngsters' at this

1 For further discussion in this area the reader is referred to McMaster, 1982.

level of interpersonal relationships are concerned, sensitive, imaginative and risk-takers. It is likely that there are as many, if not more of such people involved in intermediate treatment as in any other area of social work and education, and that it is they who are most likely to have 'success'. Therefore, although the outsider can be excused his belief that intermediate treatment is no more or no less than glorified youth clubs and the provision of treats for delinquents, it is more likely that the whole story has yet to be told about what really goes on in intermediate treatment.

In summary, intermediate treatment is finding it difficult to establish its peculiar identity within social work, education and other relevant caring disciplines, because it is unable to articulate its peculiarities. Its personnel desperately need opportunities and facilities to be more analytical and evaluative about their performance and achievement.

Current dilemmas and future challenges

Any analysis of something as tenuous and complex as intermediate treatment today is bound to raise a myriad of important issues. For example, what precisely are the roots of delinquency at which intermediate treatment is aimed to strike? If so much of juvenile delinquency and anti-social behaviour is transitory anyway, do we need to have intermediate treatment as an alternative to residential care; would a more benign and uncomplicated strategy simply be not to send offending youngsters into residential care and leave it at that? Is the diversionary nature of much intermediate treatment simply a recognition of the benign nature of delinquency, and that it will disappear anyway? Should intermediate treatment be sold as a cheap alternative to residential care? Does it need more directive leadership and clearer guidance? How can intermediate treatment and its specialists gain greater credibility within social services departments, the magistracy and police? Will the dreams of an inter-disciplinary or inter-agency approach to youngsters in difficulty or at risk ever be realised? What support systems are necessary for those in isolated and pioneering ventures at the frontiers of intermediate treatment? And so on. Therefore, any limited discussion of some of these issues, as is proposed here, necessarily demands a high degree of selectivity on the part of the writer. Four areas of significance are highlighted here.

The on-going quest for professionalism

There is much confusion in this area of professionalism related to intermediate treatment. Although throughout its development interested parties have claimed to be operating sound professional judgement, there is increasing evidence that much of it could be better described as professional interest, or what the cynic would call 'vested interest'. The magistracy would claim to be making informed judgements based on the objective evidence available; yet there is such a wide variation in how they use intermediate treatment. Social workers, together with observation and assessment centres, would claim that their recommendations are based on professional judgements; yet some areas of the country make many more recommendations for intermediate treatment than others. Social service departments and committees would claim to fix their financial priorities on the basis of an objective assessment of need; yet £150 may be spent in one area while a thousand times that figure is spent in another. Of course, it is possible that the same 'professional' criteria are being applied in the same way to all of these situations, and that the judgements which are made are in fact as professional as is possible. On the other hand, there seem to be so many variations and so arbitrarily wide, that it is difficult not to come to a conclusion either that people are defining 'professional' differently, or that something other than thorough-going professionalism is operating.

Perhaps one of the most contentious areas is the relationship between intermediate treatment and residential care. In one large social services department with a well-established intermediate treatment provision, no recommendation had gone to the Courts from the observation and assessment centres for a supervision order with an intermediate treatment condition up to the autumn of 1978. The department has stated that all recommendations are based on a thorough assessment of each child's needs, and related to resources which are available within the department and to the department. Meanwhile, in Northern Ireland, a day assessment unit was established in 1977. Only one recommendation for residential training was made out of a total of over 50 recommendations during the first half-year period (Whitefield House, Blacks Road, Belfast, Northern Ireland). It therefore becomes difficult to maintain a claim that a common, objective, informed, professional judgement was operating in such decision-making processes.

In the national investigation, intermediate treatment specialists were asked to describe their attitudes towards residential care. There were only two responses which showed a willingness to discuss its possible contribution to some youngsters with difficulties. On the other hand, there were 15 negative responses, ranging from 'a very much over-used necessary evil' to 'utterly hopeless – should be scrapped'. None of this adds anything to a picture of professional co-operation and partnership even within the departments.

It is not too difficult to hypothesise as to why there should be evidence of such a 'professional' breakdown amongst those involved in intermediate treatment, even within the same departments. In such nebulous and emotive areas as justice and care, there are so few solid milestones to tell us where we are. Facts and certainties are few and far between; indicators and trends are slightly thicker on the ground. In the main, we are left with hypotheses and hopes, theories of delinquency and research studies of deprivation. These, together with our individual value-base and level of idealism, serve to locate our individual professional stance. It is therefore small wonder that a teacher finds himself unable to communicate meaningfully with a social worker about the same child, for whom ostensibly both have the same or allied concerns. This point is emphasised throughout in this series of books on social and educational care.

The struggle for a common professionalism among caring professionals must continue. The opportunity was lost in 1969 for the creation of an integrated service to youngsters, offering an integration of concern, skills and experience. It will never be found again until a common, caring professionalism is rediscovered.

The quest for acceptance and support

It has already been noted how the more sensitive intermediate treatment specialists have been able to question the development of their service during the 1970s. Its development was hastened by the increased difficulty on the part of policy makers to accept the escalating costs of residential care. At the same time, intermediate treatment was developing alongside a far greater financial investment in secure accommodation for offending youngsters. Was intermediate treatment therefore valued for itself, or was it simply a cheap and political expedient?

The non-directive policy of development had produced at one and the same time a freedom and an uncertainty for those engaged in pioneering this new service. After 1973, there were the DHSS publications showing what had been done in some areas. The National Youth Bureau became probably a more significant resource with its regular information service and periodic publications.[1] Intermediate treatment specialists themselves formed their own national intermediate treatment forum with the aims of supporting and learning from each other. All of this support has been necessary because of the lack of clear and unambiguous guidelines and job specifications.

1 The National Youth Bureau is at 17–23 Albion Street, Leicester.

This is evidenced in the national investigation, and concluded as follows:

> The feeling that management does not understand the needs of Intermediate Treatment has already been reported, as has the frequency of negative attitudes expressed towards allied agencies and to residential care. The stated need for more training might not simply be an indictment of present professional training; it might also be a statement of present unsureness and loneliness in Intermediate Treatment. The relative absence of evaluation and feedback resources would certainly not help to assuage feelings of self-doubt and uncertainty in the sensitive Intermediate Treatment worker. There is undoubtedly a felt threat in the whole area of being an Intermediate Treatment worker working in Intermediate Treatment.

There was an expressed feeling that intermediate treatment and to a lesser extent the intermediate treatment worker had some way to go before achieving a credibility in social work and education among social workers and teachers. This degree of alienation could quite easily be the root cause of expressed loneliness, unsureness and self-doubt.

Intermediate treatment specialists were asked to state what was required before intermediate treatment would achieve what was possible for it. Their responses could be divided almost equally into two types. The first type were responses which were asking for help, e.g. training, greater management commitment, clearer DHSS support, clearer policy and role definition, and evaluation guidelines. The second type of responses was asking for greater trust to be placed in them, including additional funds being made available and a redirection of resources towards intermediate treatment. The national investigation produced a picture of an intermediate treatment service which was asking for help, for leadership and for guidance, and at the same time asking for reassurance for credibility and for acceptance.

There is now sufficient evidence to suggest that a re-evaluation of intermediate treatment strategies is necessary after 12 years of development. Aspects worthy of consideration in such a process should include a statement of clearer guidelines and leadership, the pioneering nature of much of intermediate treatment, and the 'misfit' quality of some of the best intermediate treatment personnel. And central to the whole exercise should be an attempt to identify the kinds of support systems which the specialists are crying out for.

The quest for appropriate training

The first intermediate treatment appointments reflected its three evolutionary strands, i.e. the social welfare services, the education service and the youth service. Social workers (field and residential), teachers and youth workers were appointed to intermediate treatment posts in almost equal numbers. Therefore, a service developed staffed by people of different professional stances, reflecting slightly different values and beliefs about offending and at risk youngsters and their needs. It was not long before many specialists were making noises about the need for some kind of common training specifically geared to intermediate treatment services.

This produces a complex problem and highlights the need for greater professional integration. As already mentioned, teachers, social workers and youth workers were appointed to the first flush of intermediate treatment posts in almost equal numbers. But the trend in social service departments is to favour the professionally trained social worker, that is, the holder of a Certificate of Qualification in Social Work (CQSW) as the appropriate professional for intermediate treatment. Yet, a number of recent schemes are directed by those with a background in teaching.

A possible answer to this problem may lie in the area of Post Qualifying Courses of Study recognised by the Central Council for Education and Training in Social Work (CCETSW). Although directed towards qualified social workers it is possible for teachers with appropriate experience to gain entry to some courses.

In 1977 a working party was set up in the City of Birmingham Polytechnic, including some local intermediate treatment specialists, with the task of devising a Post Qualifying Study (PQS) submission for intermediate treatment practitioners. It was recognised immediately that the primary skill needed by practitioners was the ability to work in face-to-face situations with clients, i.e. the ability to take risks in intuitive or 'natural' response. This skill development cannot normally be expected from the basic training for social workers (CQSW) or for teachers, or for youth workers. It was a difficult and new area of professional training, but perhaps at least recognised in the departing training for specialist residential child care workers. It was recommended that the experience of that specialist training (which led to the Certificate in the Residential Care of Children and Young People, but is now being phased out) be built upon in the development of PQS training for intermediate treatment.

In addition, the intermediate treatment specialists on that working party identified five problematical areas of their service for which they would be looking for a contribution of knowledge and skills in any credible training course. These areas were: the clear identification of the particular client group and their needs, realistic and valid objectives of intermediate treatment for that particular client group, the identification of usable resources and their utilisation, methodology and programming related to specific objectives, and the monitoring and evaluation of the programme. It can quickly be recognised that this covers the whole of intermediate treatment, and therefore the sooner appropriate training is available the better. There is unquestionably a need to build on and extend from the basic training of the social worker, the teacher and the youth worker engaged as a specialist on intermediate treatment programmes.

Twelve years on, intermediate treatment is at a crossroads. The possibilities and promise which were open to it in 1969 are still present, but is the will to realise them? It has the opportunity, greater than any other enactment of the 1969 legislation, of helping a confused society to rationalise the dilemma it feels. Offending youngsters need help in order not to offend again; much of their offence however may well be against an already unjust society. Therefore the help they need may not be appropriate if it is in the form of even more injustice. The role for intermediate treatment during the next decade cannot be more of the same; it must step out, with proper guidance and leadership, from behind its shell of defensiveness and sensitivity, and make a bold attempt to help a confused populace recognise that casualties, whether of war or of society, need rescuing, tending and nursing back to full health and potential. In this way, intermediate treatment may yet become what it promised, the greatest evolutionary step of this half-century in society's understanding of itself.

References

McMaster, J. McG., *Skills in Social and Educational Caring*, Gower, 1982.

More, W., *I.T. – The National Picture?*, PEPAR, 1978.

More, W., *Emotions and Adult Learning*, Saxon House, 1974.

8 The therapeutic community

JOHN D. BEGG

The therapeutic community is indebted to Maxwell Jones (1959) for its development.

> The Therapeutic Community is distinctive among other comparable treatment centres in the way the institution's total resources both staff and patients are self-consciously pooled in furthering treatment. This implies, above all a change in the usual status of patients. In collaboration with the staff they now become active participants in the therapy of other patients and in other aspects of the overall hospital work.

Clark (1965) defines the therapeutic community as:

> A small face to face residential community using social analysis as its main tool.

Martin (1963) considers a therapeutic community,

> One in which a deliberate effort is made to use to the fullest possible extent in a comprehensive plan the contribution of all staff and patients.

Of special importance for teachers and social workers involved in residential caring are four major characteristics of the method: permissiveness, democratisation, communalism and reality confrontation.

Permissiveness

Permissiveness has become such a misused and devalued word in residential child care that its use in the hearing of some practitioners can so anger them that they are unable to evaluate objectively anything else the speaker may say. Some workers avoid the use of the word altogether, replacing it with some other which has not yet lost its respectability. Bloomfield (1974) thinks 'accommodating' more appropriate in that an accommodating regime is to the child as a spectacle lens is to the eye, 'accommodating a visual defect to bring about normal vision'. It is a great pity that this has happened since the word permissive best describes this aspect of the therapeutic community. Being permissive according to the dictionary is 'granting permission or liberty'. Before granting permission or liberty, the person granting it must, presumably, be in authority or control, which is precisely the position of the director of a therapeutic community in relation to the members. The director, who is in control, permits the members to have a certain amount of his authority in relation to the control of their own conduct and holds them answerable for the manner in which they use or misuse that permission. Total permissiveness, like total freedom, does not exist, except as a philosophical concept and would have no place in residential care if it did. Yet, without permissiveness it is difficult to see how there could be a therapeutic community. Permissiveness in the therapeutic community sense is an attitude in the community which gives its members freedom to be themselves, to act out their difficulties, so that their real selves can be seen by their peers and the staff and reflected back to them in a helpful and supportive way, to enable them to overcome or come to terms with their problems. It enables children to allow their suppressed problems to come to the surface and find open expression, rather than remain hidden to be expressed covertly in more pathological and possibly more damaging ways. Freedom to act out in this way, in a community in which so many members are disturbed and disruptive, generates a considerable amount of tension and one of the staff tasks is to use this tension to further treatment (Rapoport, 1960). Permissiveness also gives children an opportunity to try out new patterns of behaviour as the old ones become less satisfying to them, thus enabling them to work through their difficulties to a new self. It must be controlled however in relation to the community's ability to handle it. When the community is functioning well and the members are working positively together and accepting a fair measure of responsibility, then they can be allowed a great deal of freedom. In times of difficulty, on the other hand, it is necessary for the director and staff to exert more control and be more overtly responsible for the functioning of the community

(Jones, 1968). It is particularly important that permissiveness is carefully regulated when dealing with disturbed children. To give them freedom they cannot handle increases their disturbance and they need to know that in times of crisis the staff are in control.

Democratisation

Democratisation may be just as difficult a concept to live with as permissiveness, for reasons which are not unrelated. Permissiveness can be interpreted as giving children freedom to do what they like; democratisation by the same token gives them the right to control the establishment, including the staff. If a school were completely democratic the children, being in the majority, would control the school, but this is not what is meant by democratisation in the therapeutic community context. Democratisation means the flattening of the hierarchical structure to enable all members of the community to have a voice in its management. Like permissiveness, it must be controlled, so that more power and responsibility may be given to the community and any areas over which the members are to have complete control are carefully worked out. To hand over to children control of, and therefore responsibility for, areas of activity for which they do not have adequate knowledge or experience to make appropriate decisions, is to put so much pressure on them that the system will break down, or the community will have to be manipulated to make the right decision, so that the whole idea of democratisation will be seen to be a sham. Either way, the result will be damaging to the therapeutic function of the establishment. It is important therefore that powers given to the community are genuine and matched to the ability of the community to handle them. Democratisation will not make life easier for anyone in the community. Staff are likely to have their traditional authority challenged and to be called upon to justify their decisions and actions, particularly if any of them, for whatever reason, are contrary to the decisions of the community. Staff will have a major part to play in monitoring the conduct of the children to ensure that they accept the increased responsibility which democratisation brings. Perhaps the most difficult thing of all for staff members in this type of regime is to know when to step into a situation and use their authority to prevent it deteriorating to the extent that children damage themselves or the building they live in. This calls for a very fine sense of judgement and timing. It should be noted that democratisation in no way relieves the staff of any part of their responsibility for the health, safety, well-being and treatment of the children; on the contrary, it adds to their responsibilities. Children in an authoritarian regime have a much easier life than those in a regime with any degree of democratisation. Having been party to a decision gives them a much greater responsibility for seeing that it is carried out. This gives them responsibility not only for their own conduct but also for that of their peers. This presents particular difficulties for children from delinquent sub-cultures where 'grassing' a friend is a grave offence, and calls for complete reorientation of ideas and values. In spite of difficulties, a degree of democratisation is indispensable to a therapeutic community.

Communalism

Communalism is probably the major factor contributing to the cohesiveness of a therapeutic community but one which causes many difficulties. While it breaks down barriers between children and staff and facilitates the formation of relationships, it is seldom total. The notion that a therapeutic community for children is completely egalitarian appears upon examination to be artificial and dishonest. There are many respects in which staff and children are not equal and this fact has to be recognised and any difficulties it raises dealt with openly. Children come to a community because, for whatever reason, they and society cannot live with each other. They have needs which the community must meet and difficulties which have to be dealt with in a way which will enable them to return to society and lead normal lives. The staff, on the other hand, come to the community because they have skills to offer to further the treatment of the children and so enter the community, whereas meeting the needs of the children is its primary function. Furthermore, the skills staff offer to the community are offered for sale, not freely given. Staff have, or should have, stable and mature personalities, while the children have usually the reverse. In terms of personality, knowledge and skill, children and staff are not equal; otherwise there would be little point in having staff. This seems to be a statement of the obvious but it is important that it should be recognised and that staff accept responsibility for their skills and superior ability, in terms of their contribution to the community.

There are other areas of difference. Children live in the community on a full-time basis; staff come and go at the beginning and end of the working day. Staff have private areas to which they can retreat from time to time. Children should also have retreat areas but they will seldom be completely out of bounds to staff. Staff also have those magic symbols of authority and superiority – keys – enabling them to have access to rooms and stores which are forbidden to children. These differences should be acknowledged and openly discussed at community meetings, for they are part of the reality of life in the community. Children will want to discuss why staff have keys, for example, and will ask whether this means that they are not trusted with free access to the areas which are locked up. The honest answer to this question must be yes; there is little point in pretending complete trust which does not exist. For instance, to trust a child who has twice taken an overdose of drugs with the key to the dispensary would not only be naive; it would be grossly irresponsible. Children in a community have to learn that trust has to be earned but should also be made aware that staff want to trust them. If the uncommunalistic bits of the relationships between children and staff are openly acknowledged and discussed they lose much of their importance and the community is free to concentrate on those areas in which there is, or should be communalism. Perhaps the most important area is that of mutual respect which seems to be essential if there is to be any communal spirit. It is also important for every member of the community to feel that he has equal rights with every other member. Feeding is also very important and separate cooking or dining facilities for staff should have no place in a therapeutic community. In short, there should be a communalistic approach to all aspects of the life of the community except where the needs of the children and the responsibilities of the staff make it impracticable or unwise.

Reality confrontation

Reality confrontation is, perhaps, even more difficult in the child care setting than in that of the psychiatric hospital. It may be necessary for the child to escape from reality for a time, in order to equip himself to face it again. One criticism of therapeutic communities is that they create an unreal environment for children, which has no validity in terms of the life they will face in the world outside. This is probably true but if the children were able to cope with the real world they would not be in the community. Some children need to be allowed to regress, to become dependent on the community for a time, before they can be helped to face the reality of life in the outside world. Cross (1975) points out that children are not prepared for bad experiences by being subjected to bad experiences. It should not be imagined that it is possible or desirable to attempt to assess the experiences which might confront a child in the future and then provide similar experiences.

> Rather our ideal will be to provide experiences, directly, therapeutic or otherwise, that promote growth, insight, freedom and dimensions of personality that ensure a future capacity for a limit-

less variety of responses appropriate to any combination of situation or experiences that may confront the individual (Cross, 1975).

One reality a therapeutic community will not allow a child to escape from is that of his own conduct and the effect it has on other people. In such a setting, more than in a traditional school, he will be required to make an appraisal of himself which may be a very painful experience and one which will be damaging unless the atmosphere in which he lives is adequately supportive. This examination of the real self, helped by peers and staff, is the reality of the therapeutic community for the child, a reality which must be faced before he will be able to face the other reality, that of the outside world. The handling of this aspect of therapeutic community life calls for a high degree of sensitivity and compassion, on the part of the children as well as the staff. When he has faced the reality of self and comes to terms with it, the child will then be ready to be helped to face other realities in his life. Treatment in this way is a long-term process, not likely to be completed in a few months.

Having looked at the four major characteristics of therapeutic communities in the context of meeting the needs of children there seems nothing in them which is inappropriate for this purpose. They are basic to the therapeutic community concept but like every other aspect of treatment, their use has to be controlled in relation to the needs and capabilities of the client group.

The level of participation required of the members of a therapeutic community is much greater than that normally expected of children in more traditional settings. This may present difficulties to children in the early stages of treatment when their attitudes will still be influenced by their sub-cultural standards. For instance, it is essential that members of a community are honest and open in their dealings with the community and this includes feeding into the community pool knowledge which they have about other members and their activities. Participation at this level presents major problems for a child whose delinquent code of conduct outlaws tale-bearing. Furthermore, this kind of co-operation with the community is inimical to the preservation of a hard delinquent image and calls for a considerable sacrifice from the child. For this reason, the new entrant to the community will only be able to participate gradually and it will be some time before he can become a fully integrated member of the community. Since progress in a personal treatment sense can only begin after this integration is achieved, this is seen as a further indication that treatment of this kind is essentially long-term.

Clearly, not all children coming into residential care will be able to benefit from the type of treatment offered in a therapeutic community proper; it is not a panacea and careful selection is necessary. Criteria for selection will vary in detail according to the circumstances of each community but there are some general factors which have to be taken into account. These include: intelligence, verbal ability, age, level of maturity, motivation, degree of identification with delinquent subculture, mental health, ability to relate to others, compatability with other members of the community, attitude of parents, sex, religion. Apart from sex and religion, there is no hierarchical significance in the order in which these factors are listed. Sex and religion are listed last because they are most easily disposed of; no debate is required. If the community is co-educational, all that needs to be established is whether there is an appropriate vacancy. If it caters for all religious persuasions, then the child's religion is irrelevant in selection terms. If it is single sex, single religion, then children of the other sex or faiths need not be considered.

The level of intelligence of the child is important for a number of reasons. Some communities are very demanding intellectually and require their members to be able to think out their problems and to gain insight into them by interaction with their peers and the staff. For this type of community, average or above average intelligence is required and a less able child would be unlikely to benefit from being placed in such a setting. Indeed, to put a child who operates at a fairly low intellectual level into such a community may be directly harmful to him. Whiteley (1970), in his research at Henderson Hospital, concluded that less mature or intelligent personalities probably became more disturbed by being in competition with their more able fellows. It is not suggested that less able children cannot benefit from a therapeutic community regime but that too wide an intelligence range in one community is unwise.

Chronological age and level of maturity need to be considered together. If a child is the right age, it will be important to discover whether he is reasonably mature or so markedly immature that he may have difficulty relating with his peers. As with intelligence, it is likely that too wide a range of maturity levels within an age group could create problems, with the less mature personalities failing to gain maximum benefit from their membership of the community. It is doubtful whether very immature children would be able to benefit from the type of treatment offered.

Motivation is very important. If a child is to persevere with treatment during the difficult times which lie ahead of him in the community he will need to be strongly motivated towards treatment. If he sees admission to the community as no more than a soft option he is unlikely to survive long enough to gain benefit from it and may harm the community in the passing. Therapeutic community treatment is a long process and a child without adequate motivation is unlikely to be willing to commit himself to a period of two, three, four, or even five years in the community.

All seriously disturbed delinquent children identify to some degree with a delinquent sub-culture but a very strong identification may be counter-therapeutic in that the child will want to hold on to his delinquent identity with which he is familiar, rather than risk giving it up in exchange for something completely unknown to him.

Brain-damaged or psychotic children are unlikely to be able to benefit from placement in a therapeutic community and their presence in the community could be damaging to it, if not to them. Research in the hospital setting suggests that neurotic adults can benefit from treatment of this kind and it is assumed that neurotic children could also benefit but much may depend on the seriousness of the neurosis. This is an area in which the writer is not qualified to comment but in general it is considered that mentally ill children should not be sent to residential child care establishments but to child psychiatry units.

Since so much of the work of a therapeutic community depends upon interaction between members, the ability to make and sustain relationships is important. Perhaps it would be more accurate to say the potential to make relationships, since a child in the early stages of treatment may have difficulties in this respect. Children who show an excessive degree of coldness may be unable to develop relationships to the necessary extent. It is because of the importance of relationships that compatability with the rest of the community is regarded as a crucial consideration in reaching a decision about the admission of a child. While compatability may not lead to the acceptance of a child, the reverse should be considered a very serious negative factor.

The importance of the parents' attitude will depend a great deal on their relationship with the child. Where the relationship is poor and the level of interest low, the child may have 'written off' his parents and their attitude will be relatively unimportant. Where there is a strong bond however the parents' attitude will be very important and they will be required to have a strong commitment to the child's treatment. Unless the parents have this commitment to the treatment programme, they may make it too easy for the child to withdraw when the going becomes difficult and he is most in need of their encouragement and support.

The selection and training of staff and the creation of an adequate support system are matters which cannot be adequately dealt with in a few paragraphs and there is only space to touch upon them here. Staff should have mature, stable and secure personalities, with a basic qualification in their own discipline which should be relevant to the work of the community. It is necessary that a candidate for a post in a community should have a strong commitment to this method of treatment and be prepared to work in the community for a number of years. It takes considerable time for a new worker to become an effective member of a community and unless he is prepared to stay for some time the community will not obtain an adequate return for the effort of integrating him. A candidate also requires to be in good physical and mental health and be able to cope with bizarre behaviour without colluding with it or being so threatened by it that he reacts inappropriately.

A work setting as stressful as a therapeutic community must have a comprehensive staff support system built into the fabric, not merely tagged on or fitted in. Regular supervision sessions with a senior colleague on a weekly basis, with extra sessions when required, will play an important part in this. It is in these sessions that the worker will be encouraged to give expression to feelings and difficulties which may be too delicate or sensitive to be discussed in public. It is important that senior staff take their role in the staff support system seriously and are constantly on the alert for signs of undue stress in their colleagues. Provision should also be made for support for senior staff. Perhaps the most important part in the staff support system will be played by the staff meeting, when members of staff will have an opportunity to discuss common problems and offer support to each other. Of almost equal importance will be the network of inter-staff relationships which should develop within the community and the mutual trust and dependency arising from these relationships. The need for staff to have time for support and supervision sessions should be one of the factors considered when determining the number of staff required to run the community.

High Plains – a therapeutic community

High Plains is a non-maintained special school under the Department of Education. The first impression gained is one of warmth and comfort. Physically, the lounge is more than comfortable; it is luxurious, with wall-to-wall carpeting, ceiling-to-floor curtains and a large log fire. This physical comfort is deliberate and has a purpose. The director and his staff believe that in treating deprived and highly disturbed children, the provision must not only be good; it must be obviously the best obtainable. Experienced residential workers may wish to debate this and to question the justification for the expense.

Warmth and comfort are not only physical feelings; they are also emotional. It is possible to feel cold in an establishment where the physical temperature is high but the emotional atmosphere is not right. This is a subjective matter, difficult to define and build into any regime but very obvious when absent. The atmosphere feels emotionally comfortable.

In keeping with the therapeutic community concept, High Plains is permissive but it is a positive controlled permissiveness, not the kind of licentious freedom often associated in the minds of the public with the word permissive. Throughout the establishment there is a strong thread of authority, without any attempt at the authoritarian use of that authority. It is very important for all children, but particularly for those who are highly disturbed, that they should feel that the adults around them can control them when they feel that they cannot control themselves. High Plains is a therapeutic community in which staff must accept their responsibilities; it is not a democracy. That is the staff view. The boys' view is much the same but is expressed differently by one of the senior boys.

> When I came here I thought I was coming to a kind of hippy commune where everyone did what he wanted to, but it isn't like that at all. There are rules and everyone, staff and boys, makes sure you obey them.

Within reasonable limits, however, it is permissive but examination of the degree of permissiveness compels thought on the whole concept of freedom. For example, a boy may sit around all day, talking to people, playing the guitar or games, or he may want to play outside and no one will interfere with him. If he has not done his share of the chores it is likely to be his peers rather than the staff who will take him to task. Similarly, he is free to say what he likes in the community meetings but what he says is likely to be interpreted and fed back to him, in a way which he may find uncomfortable or challenging. A boy is free to do what he likes, provided that in exercising that freedom he does not interfere with the freedom and rights of others or damage himself. The difference between the boy at High Plains and the ordinary citizen is that the boy, having breached the accepted rules, is not punished but helped to see the effect his conduct has on others and to understand it in terms of his own development. Freedom in High Plains terms means freedom to be yourself and to account for that self to the rest of the community.

The main vehicle for general communication is the community meeting which takes place daily between 9 a.m. and 10 a.m. by routine and on other occasions when it is considered necessary. The meeting is attended by all the boys and staff except the director, bursar, domestics and secretaries. Everyone is expected to be there on time; punctuality is important. Attendance at the community meeting is one of the obligations a boy undertakes when he agrees to come to High Plains. If he fails to come, attempts will be made to persuade him but if all else fails, he will be brought, carried bodily if necessary. Although it is the only occasion in the day when the whole community meets together, apart from meals, surprisingly little matter of a general nature comes up for discussion at the meetings attended. Even when a matter of a general nature is raised it quickly becomes focused on one boy and the difficulties being caused within the community by the nature of his relationship with another boy. The way the community meeting is able to handle such sensitive issues in the large group setting is impressive and is evidence of the concern and skill existing in the community.

Another obligation a boy undertakes on coming is a weekly meeting with his 'guru'. At first the use of the word guru to describe the member of staff particularly concerned with a boy seems ugly and jingoistic. (Guruee to describe the boy is even worse!) On second thoughts however, it seems more appropriate. None of the usual appellations given to staff in residential work seems to fit the role of the gurus. They are not care officers, houseparents, housemasters or teachers, although they may at different times be all of these. Nor are they therapists, although therapy is also part of their role. They are the key figures in the boys' treatment and have a role which is very complex and, to the outside observer, difficult to understand. Their relationship with their boys is inter-linked with their relationship with the community. Like all relationships in the community, the guru/guruee relationship is open to inspection at the community meeting and yet remains, in a sense, private. The pressures and wear and tear on the gurus is great and a new member of staff is not given a case load for the first 12 months at least. It is considered that it takes that time for the new member of staff to become sufficiently *au fait* with the community to take on this difficult task. From conversations with boys, it is clear that their relationship with their guru is very important to them and the weekly session with him or her highly valued. The weekly meeting is the minimum and boys have regular contact with their guru throughout the daily life of the community.

Education

The handling of education is one of the most unusual features. In most residential establishments, great efforts are made to motivate children to take an interest in formal education and a child can gain considerable status in the eyes of the staff by industry in the classroom. This is not the case at High Plains. Not only is there no pressure on a boy to attend classes; they are forbidden to him. Even if he expresses a desire to get involved in school-work, he is not allowed to do so. The rationale for this approach is that minds as troubled as those of the boys coming to High Plains, are not ready for learning. Time is needed for the 'kinks' to be straightened out before meaningful learning can take place. Where a 15-year-old boy has an I.Q. of 115 and a reading age of nine years, it is obvious that something is inhibiting learning. When that something is removed, boys take off in an educational sense and make nonsense of normal education system by going from, say, the standard of an 11- or 12-year-old to university entrance standard in two or three years. There is a sense in which children who are disturbed and deprived to the extent of some of those who come into residential care, can use educational activity to avoid dealing with their problems. Purposeful activity can help to remove the depression brought on by thinking about personal difficulties and most routines in residential establishments are designed to do just that. Mooning about is not allowed; the child must be active and cheerful and forget his worries. It is recognised that this approach is simply an opiate which cures nothing. There he is refused purposeful activity, is given time to think and become depressed and is denied opportunities for flight into comfortable forgetfulness. During this very difficult time he receives support from many sources, staff and older boys, community meetings and small groups, but there is no real escape from the pain that has to be lived through. This calls for a great deal of determination and courage, together with confidence that the resultant traumas can be handled without serious damage to either the child or the community. For many boys, this system appears to work very well, so that when they *are* allowed to become involved in an educational programme, they do so with outstanding success.

The style of teaching employed is more like that of a university than a conventional day school. An individual programme is made out for the boy, workshops and teaching periods are arranged but the boy himself is responsible for working to assignments, although help and encouragement are always available. The community goes to considerable trouble to ensure that a boy receives the tuition he requires. If he is studying a subject not covered by the existing staff, then arrangements can be made for a visiting teacher to instruct him on a sessional basis. By this means, the range of subjects is much wider than would normally be available in a residential establishment.

As in most living situations the preparation and eating of food is organised so that the utmost therapeutic value is derived from it. The emotional significance of food for deprived and disturbed children is recognised in the way it is prepared and presented. It is cooked by two boys and two members of staff and served by them to the other members of the community on a cafeteria system. All the members take turns at carrying out this duty. The food is of good quality and the quantity is more than adequate. Mealtimes are something of a ritual. Everyone must attend and any boy who is missing will be sent for and, if necessary, brought to the dining room. Once there he may refuse to eat but he must be present. Tables are always 'properly' set, with the cutlery appropriate to the meal laid out in the right way, with nothing out of place. Food costs are high but no one at High Plains doubts that the money is well spent. It is interesting to reflect on the fact that there are few people in residential work with children who doubt the emotional importance of food, yet it is one area where establishments are always under pressure to cut costs, or at best, keep them strictly under control. It is as though the only function of feeding children is to provide the right amount of proteins and carbohydrates at the lowest possible unit cost.

One of the striking features of the community, to this writer, is the attitude of the boys. The senior boys, who have been there for four or five years, express a deep commitment to the community. They recognise the great benefit they have had from their stay and, in their final months in the community, seem to want to make a contribution to the treatment of the younger boys. This positive attitude can be seen in the way they speak to other boys, who may be indulging in inappropriate conduct likely to be damaging to themselves or the fabric or furnishings. The older boys feel they can offer as much to the new boys as the staff, or perhaps more, since they have been through what the others are still going through and know how they feel. The younger boys appear to appreciate that the older ones are trying to be helpful and respond fairly positively to advice, most of the time. The attitude of the younger boys is also positive, even when they are having a bad time and things are not going well. There seems to be a recognition that everything in the place, even the parts they do not like, is geared towards their rehabilitation.

The impression gained by the writer is that it is an establishment where an extremely difficult task is being tackled by a staff who have given a great deal of thought to what they are about and have acquired a great deal of skill in running a therapeutic community for their particular client group. The present stability in the community has been hard earned and the staff are aware that it could be so easily lost. As to the value to its clients, that is best summed up in the answer given by a 15-year-old when asked whether he thought it would help him. 'I think it might, Christ it better or I'm finished, nothing else has worked for me.'

The director and staff would be the last people to claim that they have created or adapted a system which is a model for others to follow. They have taken the method of the therapeutic community and adapted it to meet the needs of their particular client group, which is carefully selected. Boys admitted to High Plains, while grossly disturbed, are of above average intelligence. What can be learned from High Plains is that the method of the therapeutic community will work in the field of residential child care, provided the work is well thought out and planned with the needs of the particular client group in mind. Staff have to have a very firm grip on reality and a clear view of their aims. Woolly, sentimental thinking is a recipe for disaster. A final word with the director:

> Perhaps many permissive experiments fail because they are not based on any initial stability but on uncertainty and on an atmosphere of experiment.

References

Bloomfield, A.W., 'A Therapeutic Community for Adolescent Boys, Part I', *Residential Social Work*, vol.14, no.6, pp. 171-2, June 1974.

Clark, D.H., 'The Therapeutic Community – Concept, Practice and Future', *Br. Jrnl. of Psychiatry*, vol.111, pp. 947-54, 1965.

Cross, J., 'Therapeutic Communities', *Jrnl. of the Assoc. of Workers for Malad. Children*, vol.3, no.1, pp. 20-26, 1975.

Jones, M., 'Towards a Clarification of the Therapeutic Community Concept', *Br. Jrnl. of Med. Psychology*, vol.32, no.3, pp. 200-5, 1959.

Jones, M., *Social Psychiatry in Practice*, Penguin, Harmondsworth, 1968.

Martin, D.V., Quoted by Clark in 'Administrative Psychiatry', *Br. Jrnl. of Psychiatry*, vol.109, pp. 178-201, 1963.

Rapoport, R., *Community as Doctor*, Tavistock, London, 1960.

Whiteley, J.S. 'The Response of Psychopaths to a Therapeutic Community', *Br. Jrnl. of Psychiatry*, vol.116, pp. 17-29, 1970.

9 A personal view of groupwork

JACK B. RONALDSON

Groupwork is a valuable and important method of social and educational caring. It is used by social workers and teachers in different settings. There are many definitions of groupwork as a method; here it is presented as that form of groupwork referred to as *intensive group experience*.

The purpose of this chapter is to help the reader to plan and set up a group, tell how to lead it, what difficulties are likely to be encountered and how to tackle them. It is written from a background both academic and practical, but emphasis is on personal experiences using the method. This experience includes working with children and adults; normal and special schools; youth clubs; the training of teachers, social workers, and youth leaders; and work with such voluntary organisations as the National Marriage Guidance Council and the Pre-school Playgroups Association. The problems which have emerged from these experiences are those which the reader is also likely to meet. A typical example is where the group leader plans a session and no one speaks. This may lead to immediate panic.

Aims and objectives of groupwork

There are three basic objectives which can be met by this method. First, group discussion encourages self-expression in children and young people. While the method is applicable to any age group it becomes more relevant with adolescents. As part of their essential growth towards adulthood they must form a sense of self-identity, and the self-expression which is encouraged in groups helps the adolescent reach more autonomous decisions and formulate his own morality.

Second, successful groupwork promotes the sharing and, hence, alleviation of personal anxieties. For the adolescent these anxieties stem from the rapid changes in physical and social development, as well as from career development. If not expressed at the period when they arise, the unresolved anxieties are carried into adulthood.

Third, the group experience promotes good relationships between peers, between teacher and children, social worker and clients. When people are encouraged to express difficulties in interpersonal relationships and the feelings attached to these breakdowns in communication openly, then the problems can be resolved. When two people or factions agree to differ, everyone knows where they stand, and can take suitable avoiding action. The establishment of clear and positive communication between peers is an original and valuable learning experience for everyone.

There are other aims for groupwork which are no less important. Groupwork provides young people with an opportunity to experience freedom from classroom restrictions for discussion, in the presence of a warm and caring group leader. There is freedom to discuss those topics which interest them, matters which arise from their needs. In a competitive society, which is mirrored in schools, there is in groupwork a welcome opportunity to experience co-operation and cohesion between members.

Applications

Groupwork is a method which can be applied in many settings, for example in high schools both in subject teaching and in pastoral care. In sex education or personal relationship courses where free but safe discussion of sensitive issues is essential, the method of groupwork can be invaluable. It has been practised successfully in schools for the maladjusted ranging from the problems of living together to deeper and personal anxieties. A colleague has used the method successfully in a local community home with a group of glue sniffers. In youth clubs it has been used to provide opportunities for discussion of such diverse topics as under-age drinking, parents, homosexuality and why the billiard table is always torn. There is little logic in the order of topics which arise but this is to be welcomed.

Groupwork is also appropriate in intermediate treatment settings when increased insight into the young person's behaviour is the objective.

In the voluntary sector group discussion is an essential feature of organisations such as Alcoholics Anonymous, Gingerbread and Mind. Self-help organisations are based on a fundamental premise that people can help each other, and the non-hierarchical structure of the group lends itself to this use. Groupwork is relevant wherever there exists an important need for people to learn to communicate with each other. Society seldom encourages or teaches interpersonal skills, and it is often only on breakdown in adolescence and adulthood that the need to learn to relate to others is recognised and acted on.

All of us need increased effectiveness in interpersonal relationships. In this context groupwork can be used for discussion, personal growth, therapy, training in interpersonal communication and for combinations of these.

Planning to set up a group

In planning to set up a group it is important to bear in mind reasons and personal motives for introducing groupwork, aims for members and for the school or club, whom to consult and inform, as well as more mundane matters such as size, structure and location. There is no single approach to cover all eventualities; hence the need to build up one's own group experience to satisfy the requirements of the specific circumstances. A fuller account of the 'rules' for establishing a group are given by Hodge (1977). Readers are also referred to an excellent check list on planning given in Douglas (1976, pp. 41-2).

Reasons and motives

It is important to consider carefully where the motivation has come from. Is this personally instigated as a result of training and interests or is it imposed externally by an administrator, headmaster or a total organisation? Where the method is being imposed on reluctant group leaders, it is better that some other method be used, or some other member of staff be used as leader, for poor motivation will lead to poor results and spurious if not damaging behaviour in the group. While personal interest in groupwork is essential for the leader, it is also important that this interest be harnessed to the perceived needs of the agency.

It is not easy to lead groups and there must be interest and motivation on the part of the leader. A group with a leader who is half-hearted about the method will not be successful. Groupwork is never the routine administration of a set of techniques to a group of people, and it is essential that the personality and motivations of the leader be appropriate.

It is important to be clear about the aims for the group members, the aims for the organisation and to consider how far these are consistent with each other.

With groups of young people the expressed aim is often 'exploring personal relationships'. This may be a euphemism for sex education, or it may be the teaching of those aspects of sex education which exclude 'the plumbing'. Most likely settings for groups of young persons are schools, community homes or youth clubs. It is usually more difficult to set up groups in schools, where *affective* education plays a minor part in the curriculum of the majority of schools. Young people have little guidance in the handling or discussion of the social and emotional difficulties which arise in the course of adolescence.

Some groups will be set up solely for therapeutic purposes. These run from group psychotherapy in hospital settings to the variety of personal growth or sensitivity training groups in the human potential movement. The aim of the latter is to help normal people to develop their resources and thus live fuller and happier lives.

The needs of the organisation will not necessarily be consistent with the aims expressed above. Be wary of expressed organisational aims such as 'to foster a community spirit in the school' when the covert aim is to persuade young people to conform to a specific set of rules, e.g. to stop smoking in the toilets, or reduce alcohol intake in the youth club. It is devious and dishonest to use the trust-building framework of the group to feed in pre-determined ideas, as opposed to encouraging young people to attain some degree of autonomous morality.

Size and location

There is much discussion of the optimum size of groups and the writer has worked successfully with groups of different sizes. There is, however, general agreement that between 8 and 16 is acceptable. Carl Rogers (1978) has talked of working with a large group of 600 to 800, and breaking these into 'small' groups of 100! This is exceptional. Where numbers fall below eight, there is a risk of individual conversations developing between leader and members, or the group running out of energy if interests are similar. Groups above 16 tend to become public meetings where the leader spends much time playing chairman.

Size and location are obviously interrelated and it is important to decide both in advance. Larger groups need larger rooms with a consequent reduction in acoustics and comfort. Corners of draughty public halls are not ideal locations for easy interaction. Locations will vary in atmosphere and hence degree of ease felt by members. The atmosphere of the headmaster's study with associations of 'being sent for' may hinder conversation, while on the other hand a group held in informal settings such as round a table in the local club disco will not achieve much because of the distractions.

Consultation and information

Where groupwork is being introduced as a result of the leader's interests, good public relations are especially important. It is not easy to explain groupwork in detail but some attempt should be made to gain the co-operation and goodwill of the agency involved. Where this agreement is not forthcoming, it should be seriously questioned whether to continue. There are always repercussions on the organisation, one of the more obvious being the difference between those who have shared the experience and those who have not. Such differences may threaten existing working relationships within the organisation, if not carefully anticipated and prepared for.

Composition

Having thought carefully about reasons, aims, size and consultation, the next step is to determine the membership. An early decision to be made is whether the group is voluntary or compulsory, for this will affect the degree and nature of participation. The imposition of group discussion in a youth club setting would be difficult to achieve in any case, when members would simply vote with their feet, but such a degree of choice in participation is unusual in schools or where a child is in care. Intermediate treatment groups may be mandatory. As in individual counselling or casework, the unwilling client is not a good prospect for beneficial change.

The aims and objectives which have been agreed earlier will often determine the other variables of composition, but the following questions should be asked:

1 What age group is wanted, and should the members be of similar or differing ages? It should be said that group methods are easier with older verbal adolescents, and with adults, than with shy 13-year-olds. The pre-teens are also good material, but require more control. Mixed age groups may learn from each other or ignore each other, especially if the age gap is large.

2 Mixed or single sex? Sex distribution is not important in pre-teen or in adult groups, unless the purpose of the group is gender-linked (e.g. women's rights group). However, in the adolescent period, where more issues are sensitive to the members concerned, sex distribution is a crucial factor. The nature of the discussion of relationships with the opposite sex will be determined by the presence or absence of members of the opposite sex.

3 Personality types? It is less easy to pre-select for personality type than it is for age and sex. People are heterogeneous. It is unlikely to obtain a group in which all are shy and silent, or all active participants. However, if there is some choice in the matter of selection by personality, it is suggested a mixture of types is best. Groups set up for timid adolescents who do not participate are unproductive and a structured approach such as social skills training may be more advantageous.

Setting

A desirable setting is a medium-sized carpeted room with 8 to 12 easy chairs arranged in a circle. The chairs should be comfortable, for it is not easy to sit on a hard, upright wood or metal chair for an hour. Where the room is carpeted, in less formal organisations, consider sitting on the floor on cushions.

Arrange the chairs informally, preferably in a circle. This allows everyone to see each other and accords no status to the group leader, as do rows or semi-circles with the leader out in front. Again though not essential, it is helpful to have an 'empty centre', i.e. that the centre of the circle should not be filled with coffee tables. These can easily be positioned slightly behind the chairs and are thus less obtrusive. As in office desks between manager and employee or doctor and patient, the effect of furniture is symbolic. One can hide behind a coffee table as one can hide behind spectacles or cigarettes!

Number of meetings, and times of starting and finishing, should be agreed either beforehand or early on in the group. It is then clear to all that, for example, the group meets every Wednesday morning from 9.30 to 10.30 for six weeks. Groups which amble on from week to week become irritating and confusing, for towards the end of each session there is usually a long discussion about whether to meet again or not.

Deciding the timing of meetings helps members' commitment to the group experience, and this may need to be looked at if group numbers begin to fall over the weeks. Is absence due to the current 'flu' epidemic, antagonism to the leader, lack of skill? These are some of the doubts which are likely to assail the leader when members do not come back.

Interruptions are a constant source of frustration especially in some schools and most youth club settings. It is not always possible to avoid having a pneumatic drill outside or a violin class next door, but it is worth the effort in the long run to make protestations in the appropriate quarters about such interruptions. It is useful to decide procedures such as having a 'Do not disturb' notice on the door, or that telephones be ignored or disconnected. Personal experiences in schools suggest that each has a number of children with messages who knock on all classroom doors at 10-minute intervals throughout the day! Groups will often decide for themselves how to deal with situations like these.

Content

Several theoretical approaches to groupwork exist and it should be decided in advance how one intends to lead. Some of these approaches are described by Douglas (1976). The assumption there is that in most instances the groups to be organised by the reader will be groups of young people where the emphasis will be on current concerns and present interactions in the group.

An early decision to be taken by the leader is how much structure to impose on the group. At one end of the continuum is the T-group approach where the leader remains impassively silent while the members sort out their own structures and agenda. This is a risky exercise with young people. On the other hand too much structure in the sessions with exercises and controls allows little individual freedom for the members. A compromise arrangement is to introduce an exercise such as a round of the circle where everyone in turn says who they are, where they live and what they think about school or work. This will normally produce enough controversial material for the others to wish to join in, and a natural discussion will ensue. Rapid adaptability is a key quality in a skilled group leader and he should be ready to introduce further structured exercises when discussion falters. A useful set of such exercises in handy format is a book by Brandes and Phillips (1977).

Having brought the group together in a suitable place, how does one start? There is no fixed pattern for starting groups but this writer likes to include some or all of the following: explaining purposes, setting times, guidelines or principles and introductions.

It is important to explain clearly and simply the object of meeting together. It is important to introduce oneself, especially if from outside the organisation, and why there has been the invitation to do this work. The timing and number of sessions can then be outlined and comments asked for on these practical arrangements and any others which arise.

As mentioned earlier it is important to provide some guidelines or basic principles for group behaviour. It is difficult to be free when there are no rules, whether in a small group situation or in the wider society. Most of us cannot cope with total freedom, and when no rules are given, groups will spend their time making up their own rules. This may be a valuable exercise if this is the purpose of the group, but it is more helpful and ethical to provide a set of guidelines. There is much mystery surrounding groups and these guidelines provide a number of reassuring anchor points. It is normal to provide some or all of the following and each leader should choose those he feels happy with: pointing out that starting and finishing times will be adhered to, whether members may leave the group at any times and under what circumstances, no physical violence, support rather than adverse criticism of other people, confidentiality outside the group, tolerable noise levels, role of the leader. Two examples of these guidelines may be helpful.

Confidentiality is always a tricky problem. It is easy to say that no one should talk about other group members outside the group sessions. However, people like to talk about others and this is an impossible condition to meet. Personal experience suggests that people talk outside anyway and the rule simply provides a source of guilt. It is better to express these doubts about confidentiality directly to the members. This is honest, in that it does not seduce people into revealing innermost secrets under a guarantee that these revelations will remain secret. Better to ask people to take responsibility for what they wish to reveal and to be aware that what they say may be repeated outside. Where there are implications for school or for existing relationships, it may be better not to reveal what appears to be compromising information. The sense of relief at talking about some misdemeanour or negative feeling may be quickly counterbalanced and obliterated by later losing one's status or one's friend through gossip. It is important that people bear this in mind before they act.

A second guideline which may create discussion is the one about supporting rather than criticising. How can people help each other if they do not pick out their faults and bring them to attention? One answer is that most of us are perfectly aware of our shortcomings, as these will have been pointed out frequently in the past. What we cannot do is admit them, to ourselves or to others, in case we are no longer loved and approved. When this love and support is given by other group members, it is then that we can admit to the negative aspects of ourselves and initiate ways of changing these. It is not a question of ignoring the shortcomings and pretending they do not exist. It is more like being aware that the faults exist and patiently waiting until the person is ready to talk about them, in his own good time, not ours. This is a very difficult thing to do, for we are wedded to the idea that in the end telling one's friend about his b.o. is the most helpful thing we can do.

Having outlined purposes and guidelines, it is important to get members participating as quickly and as smoothly as possible. The introduction exercise mentioned earlier in this section is a good way to do this. Biographical information like names, domicile and school class are easy to remember, and should not require too much courage to state in public, even for the most shy. Brief and neutral comments by the leader are welcome, if appropriate, and naturally introduce some two-way interaction between leader and members. Questions which are likely to produce deeper self-disclosure or reticence are best avoided at this stage. For example, 'Does your father not live at home then?'

Free discussion may follow this round of introductions, but if not, the leader may pick up points from some of the contributions if they are relevant to the stated objectives of the group. Topics which interest young people will vary according to age, region, or what is currently in the news, but certain topics never fail to catch interest. Examples of these are boy friends and girl friends, relationships with parents, finding a job or being at work for the first time, the difficulties of growing up and teenage problems picked from a letters page in a magazine. If possible the topics should arise from the group rather than be imposed by the leader.

Discussion in the early stages will fluctuate wildly from topic to topic until something takes the group's deeper interest and they settle on it. The leader should resist the temptation to have an ordered discussion, for it is unnatural – other than in formal debate – for any discussion to reach a conclusion. Where discussion is too diffuse on the other hand, some gentle leading back to the topic may be wise.

Role and functions of leader

The principal function of the group leader is to create an atmosphere or climate of trust and tolerance which will allow or encourage members to speak openly and spontaneously about their attitudes, prejudices, needs or desires. He is also there to help the group gently along the way it wishes to go, to encourage the shy and restrain the over-vociferous. These are no easy tasks, but challenging ones which demand a degree of observation, listening and sensitivity, as well as a certain humility which will allow the leader to merge quietly into the background when not needed.

On first hearing a colleague say 'Give them what they want', it was difficult to accept that people could know better than the writer what they wanted or needed for their development. Many years' personal experience confirm that this is no mean principle to apply to group members, to individual clients, to pupils or students. This is not self-abasement or a denial of the important role played in helping or teaching others, but sure knowledge based on experience that when trying to do otherwise, by taking over responsibility for what people need, failure results. There is a devaluing of the group members in assuming they do not know what is best for them. It also encourages undue dependency on the leader as the wise one who will know all the answers and help them see the light or reach nirvana. This is a seductive invitation for the group leader.

It may be helpful at times to comment on what is happening within the group itself (e.g. 'it looks as if people are finding it difficult to cope with what is happening just now'). This may release some block in communication in the group. If in doubt whether to comment or not, do not, for you may easily produce intellectual confusion, and hinder the flow of interaction.

It is impossible to advise on the amount of intervention or control by the leader. This will depend on factors such as age and personality. Younger children require more intervention if the group is not to break into a melee, while older people are better able to impose their own controls and allow others a chance to speak. The main function is to facilitate discussion, and this facilitation may be achieved by taking direct control of the situation or by quietly keeping out of the way.

It is appropriate at this point to mention the pitfalls for a group leader, especially the dilemma of amount of initiative to take. There are two extremes: one is taking too little initiative and leaving everything vague, especially in the early stages. This creates confusion, then mistrust of the leader, which may get in the way of more useful learning. The alternative trap is believing there is so much that the leader can *teach* the members and that time is short. This is unfortunate, for, as Lieberman and his colleagues (1973) state: 'Change does not revolve around the solitary sun of the leader . . . ' (p.428).

Interactions between group members play an exceedingly important part in the process of individual change, and the leader may block these exchanges in attempting to satisfy his own needs for charisma. There are, however, other times when it is positively harmful if the leader does not intervene. One member may be trying to get in and say something, or may have said something personal which the others do not find appealing to take up at that point. It may be necessary to move gently in and encourage that person to continue and the group to listen. This is, however, similar to attempts at social engineering in schools and youth clubs where the intention is to make a child more integrated with the others. They may allow the child to play with them for a while to please you then reject him and carry on with the real business of their lives. Sensitivity to the people concerned is more important than any rule-of-thumb technique in dealing with situations like these.

Common problems and how to deal with them

One of the most frightening experiences for the inexperienced group leader is silence. Common feelings are panic, apprehensiveness, and the thought that silence must be filled, at all costs. It feels dreadful sitting in a circle with everyone's eyes to the floor, and people shuffling around, hoping the leader will do something, in the same way that the traditional teacher or social worker would to get things going. A 30-second silence in those circumstances can feel like a lifetime, and it is probable that the leader will wish he had not embarked on the method of groupwork. Be reassured; these are common experiences in the early stages of a group's life, until sufficient trust slowly builds up and allows members to open up and express their thoughts and feelings.

Silence in a group may be caused by unexpressed anger and resentment, by lack of trust that whatever is expressed will be accepted by the leader or the other members, or more simply by lack of information. The silent member does not know what is expected of him. It is common to sit in groups, wondering what to say, whether it will be pleasing to the leader, whether the contribution will help others, or create resentment against self. The usual result of all this mental meandering is to block and say nothing.

The role of the leader is to help members think about what they are saying and about the possible consequences in taking the risk of saying it. Where the risk is too great and leads to mental gymnastics and silence, then the risk needs to be reduced by the introduction of simpler and less threatening topics by the leader. A common failing is to push too quickly into deeper material, and almost force people into silence. It is normal to feel insecure and paranoid when faced with a group of silent people, and think that they are doing it intentionally. The tendency at that point is to become defensive and incompetent and to provoke some reaction by needling and confronting individuals. It is better to close the session early and discuss it with a supervisor before starting again. Stopping early is not a failure of the group experience.

What can be done about silence depends on the perception of the cause. When this is lack of information about the leader's expectations then he may gently remind members that the group has been set up for them to talk about anything they wish, or to remain silent if so desired, and check with them that silence is what they genuinely want at this time. From personal sensitivity one can often feel the quality of the silence and decide if it is a relaxed and peaceful experience or bottled up anger. If the latter, it may be appropriate to bring this out by saying 'It feels like there is quite a lot of anger around here today' without identifying anyone. This should be said in a gentle manner to convey the message that this is acceptable and that anger is a normal emotional response. In the later stages of a group's life you may be able to help members express their anger in a safe, non-violent way.

Contingencies

This leads to the problem of how to handle emotional blow-ups such as anger, tears, walking out, verbal attack or physical aggression.

Anger or aggression blow-ups are easier for the teacher to handle, for there is always the back-up of his physical powers of restraint or those of other adults in the vicinity, if the worst comes to the worst. However, this type of powerful clamp-down on emotions is not necessarily the most helpful way of dealing with the situation, either for the individual involved or for the others. What they see is that aggression will be met by aggression, and this can reinforce ideas that the strongest always wins.

It may be helpful if the leader allows the anger to be expressed by shouting or by giving the member a cushion to beat until the anger dissipates or resolves into another emotion, commonly tears of laughter from sheer exhaustion. To remind members of the guideline that no physical violence is allowed would be appropriate. If a member does physically attack another member or the leader, there should be no hesitation in restraining the person, preferably with the co-operation of some of the stronger members of the group. When this has been done discussion should ensue on why the attack happened, and what alternative ways might have been open to the person concerned.

Crying produces much embarrassment for the member concerned and for the others. People wish to help by cheering the person up, or by providing tissues or cups of tea. It often engenders accusations by all except the person concerned that the leader has 'made' her cry, and how cruel he is. The reason for the tears is often a sense of security and relief that she can trust the group enough to release her tension. Younger children are less able to articulate such experiences. It is normal here to allow the child to weep gently, and make reassuring gestures to everyone that it is natural to cry and there is nothing to worry about. A box of paper tissues is a handy first-aid kit for the group leader. When the weeping has stopped and the conversation may have changed direction, the leader should remember that the child will still be feeling vulnerable. It is important to make the child feel part of the group again by bringing her back into another conversation at a later time.

Dealing with emotions in the group is a contingency which can be frightening to the inexperienced groupworker. The possibility of an angry blow-up between members, or a strong attraction, or a flood of tears can easily send the leader scurrying into the safer waters of verbal interchanges and intellectualising in order to defuse the perceived threat to the group or to himself. However, these safety nets or escape routes are not helpful to the individuals concerned, for this is how their friends and colleagues outside the group will have probably treated their expressed emotions in the past. The individual therefore is seldom allowed the opportunity to explore in depth the emotions which he feels. The well-functioning group will provide the necessary warmth and support to allow the member to experience his emotions as a natural part of his personality. As part of his own training in groupwork, the leader who cannot cope easily with emotional situations must work on his own emotional blocks in his consultations with a colleague or supervisor experienced in groupwork.

Recording and evaluation

Groupwork sessions can be recorded on audio or video-tape either partially or in full, by check-lists or by less structured verbal descriptions of the experience by members or the group leader. Audio recording provides a complete account of verbal content and intonation, while video-recording adds the non-verbal quality. However, there can be disadvantages of technical quality, loss of range, and the chore of replaying the tapes to transcribe or summarise the content. The presence of the equipment, especially with video, will certainly influence and may well hinder the interactive process. For this writer mechanical recording is not helpful, except when training group leaders when discussion of content with the trainee can be valuable. For discussion in this area the reader is referred to McMaster (1982).

Douglas (1976) gives a series of suggestions, check-lists and questionnaires containing questions such as 'What was the general atmosphere in the group?' followed by a list of adjectives to tick off ('formal', 'competitive', 'hostile', etc.). These can be useful memory aids, but constrictive and limited when attempting to grasp the essential quality of the group experience.

A less structured method of recording is to ask members to write down what they thought was happening in the group and how they felt about these events. This can be done by asking members to keep a journal of their experiences, week by week. In the past these recordings have proved personally useful. The ability of young people to write of their personal experiences is often underestimated. Naturally the number and quality of members' records varies, especially if the recording is not compulsory, and therefore there is an incomplete picture of the experience. However, a composite picture will always be incomplete since it is made up of many individual experiences which are only vaguely transmitted by the limitations of the language available.

A helpful approach is to sit down within 24 hours after the event and attempt to describe the experience, knowing all the limitations of language, selective memory and personal prejudices and interests. Recording should be divided into content and process. Content recording is self-explanatory. Process recording is the interpretation of what was happening for the leader and other members beneath the surface of the verbal content. It is the world of feelings, needs, wishes, rejections, hopes, sympathies, anger and irritation. It is hopelessly irrational and unprovable. It will contain an account of how the leader, say, was feeling annoyed with a particular member and the tentative reason for this. Was it appearance or behaviour? A reminder of a past event? This activity helps to focus attention on experiences in the group, which will influence leader behaviour. Process recording is a way of increasing awareness of the leader's interpersonal behaviour. The sharing of this level of recording has been personally useful and for trainees rather than long accounts of who said what to whom. It is especially useful to re-read recordings before the next meeting to key into what was being experienced previously.

Evaluation

Strict evaluation of the effectiveness of a particular group and of groupwork is fraught with methodological difficulties. Whether or not a particular group experience has been effective is a very individual question, and adding the experiences of 12 people together and then averaging out masks the essential quality of individual experience.

As in research on the effectiveness of psychotherapy, the two principal difficulties are what criterion of 'success' to employ; and what instruments to use in order to measure before and after effects. The two difficulties are of course linked: if it is decided that 'better interpersonal skills' is the criterion of effectiveness, a reliable and valid measure of interpersonal skills must be found. A very useful attempt at assessing effectiveness of different types of group has been made by Liebermann, Yalom and Miles (1973).

Simple criteria such as members' views are interesting. One member summed up a weekend group as, 'Overall, a very valuable and warm experience, a source of strength and a focus for thinking and appraisal which was most welcome'. Given our present state of knowledge of psychological measurement, it is better to maintain this type of personal evaluation than to pretend that numbers from computer analysis data are more meaningful, because they have an air of scientific respectability.

Conclusions

This chapter has been a statement of those principles found to be important in setting up and leading a group. The view is a personal one and each leader will develop his own style. The contention is that there are certain advantages which groupwork possesses over other methods of social and educational caring. Working in a group is often more acceptable than individual caring, which may be too intense. It is easier in the larger group to come forward and talk, and then to merge quietly into the background. Second, groupwork is less expensive on time and resources than individual helping. Eventually the skills of caring are learned by members as they watch others helping. Third, it is often easier to begin to demonstrate caring in a group which has originally been set up for a different purpose.

Groupwork is a method of wide applicability which requires strength and skills in the leader; skills which are not readily acquired, and many give up. Yet the benefits from sharing and supporting in a group setting are long-term; experienced people are likely to continue to express future worries and so receive reassurance and help. In a wider perspective society has an obligation to teach communication and caring skills. Groupwork can go a long way towards this obligation.

References

Brandes, D. and Phillips, H., *Gamesters' Handbook*, Hutchinson, London, 1977.

Douglas, T., *Groupwork Practice*, Tavistock, London, 1976.

Hodge, J., 'Social groupwork rules for establishing the group', *Social Work Today*, vol.8, no.17, 1 February 1977, pp. 8-11.

Lieberman, M.A., Yalom, I.D. and Miles, M.B., *Encounter Groups: First facts*, Basic Books, New York, 1973.

McMaster, J. McG. (ed.), *Skills in Social and Educational Caring*, Gower Publishing Co., 1982.

Rogers, C.R., 'Some new directions: A personal view', unpublished 1978.

10 Postscript
JOHN McGREGOR McMASTER

Five methods which have significance for teachers, social workers and others have now been covered; assessment, behaviour modification, intermediate treatment, the therapeutic community and groupwork.

Appropriate methods should enable the professional to achieve what he wants to do. In this sense *method* should only be a means to an end. For example, assessment may become important solely for collecting information which becomes an end in itself. Teachers, social workers, psychiatrists and psychologists are sometimes prone to this syndrome which is often a defence against inadequate knowledge and ability. If data remain sterile they are worthless; certainly worthless for the child or client. It should become an integral part of treatment or education. Assessment as an ongoing process should affect the child as a total person (Warnock, 1978). In chapter 3, O'Connor says:

> But pupils are human beings not to be programmed by mechanistic methods alone. Such methods, though logically based, give results which are incomplete because they disregard the influence of the emotions upon learning (p.29).

When dealing with human beings the importance of feelings needs to be emphasised.

Behaviour modification is often abused when charts, graphs and complicated schedules become the end product. The programmer becomes programmed and is positively reinforced each time information is recorded. But this should be secondary to using the method to solve the presenting difficulty.

A recurring problem is initial over-enthusiasm to show how successful the method can be. Undue haste prevents the objective being achieved, at the expense of the child or client.

Being professional is an extremely responsible business. This is not the same as being called a professional. Having the label teacher or social worker gives an identity but it does not automatically mean good professional practice. Essential ingredients are knowledge, method and skill with the appropriate admixture of these for specific problems (see p.9).

Part of the task should be to contribute to and improve method but too often trust is placed in a method simply because it is there. This is not enough. Similar points are made in CCETSW[1] (1980) which also acknowledges the 'current uncertainty about the appropriateness and effectiveness of different modes of intervention'.

More (p.100) reminds us that: 'the struggle for a common professionalism among caring professionals must continue'. In this context his reference to teachers running a programme of social learning for truants and classroom disruptors is apt.

Intermediate treatment as method was mainly influenced by political expediency, a poor substitute for rigorous research. Combing learned journals for research findings which help establish good method in the caring professions often produces disappointment and disillusionment. Yet, systematically developed methods are vitally important for the practising teacher and social worker.

Queries often crop up concerning the mixing of methods in treatment and education. Sometimes methods are incompatible because of differing underlying rationales, as for example in behaviour modification and 'T' group work. It is the professional's responsibility to understand the rationale upon which methods are based and select the most suitable. There should be strong commitment to the method practised together with a firm belief in its efficacy. In describing the therapeutic community Begg makes this clear:

> It is necessary that a candidate for a post in a therapeutic community should have a strong commitment to this method of treatment and be prepared to work in the community for a number of years (p. 112).

Methods are undoubtedly important. It would, therefore, seem logical to turn to training and courses which equip students with the

1 Central Council for Training and Education and Social Work.

methods to be practised. If a course of professional training is offered by an institution it is reasonable to expect that knowledge, methods and skills appropriate to that profession will be learned. If this is not achieved then it is legitimate to view the training with scepticism.

Teacher training has frequently been criticised on the grounds of not providing a link between theory and practice; of not spending enough time on appropriate methods and skills (Morrison and McIntyre, 1975). Entwistle (1974) from his interviews with lecturers and students found 'serious inadequacies in the current system'.

One difficulty is in the staffing of courses and their organisation. For example, methods lecturers and tutors rarely meet with the psychologists, philosophers, sociologists and others. The tutor may often have much experience of the classroom and pass on sound practical guidance, but the guidance may lack rigorous theoretical application from the relevant discipline, e.g. psychology. The psychologist, on the other hand, may only be concerned with the students' knowledge of psychological theories and be unable or unwilling to link this to practice. The net result is a polarisation of view created by the establishment.

A different approach is where all lecturers take a share in the contributing disciplines. This can produce the equally unsatisfactory state where experienced tutors become quasi-sociologists, psychologists or philosophers.

There are signs that some courses are taking a long and serious look at how they operate and much more realistic attempts are being made in the direction of professionalism.

Social work training is in a state of upheaval and uncertainty. Much of the blame for this rests with the CCETSW, the British Association of Social Workers (BASW), and the training courses.

The guidelines laid down by CCETSW for the CQSW are full of generalisations and singularly unhelpful. In reviewing 40 courses for the CQSW, Hayward (1979) makes the point:

> Though there is talk of a body of essential knowledge students themselves seem confused about what it is and whether they have acquired it at the end of the course.

She also emphasises problems common to social work and education and suggests the possibility 'for parallel developments within the colleges'.

BASW is experiencing much bickering and strife over status in social work, not least being the argument over accreditation.

Training should *guide* the effective application of method in social work; a point discussed at length by Millham, Bullock and Hosie (1980).

A personal view is that teaching and social work could and should become high status professions, even though systematic, effective and efficient methods are, currently, hard to find. The 1980s will see a move towards more specificity, objectivity and a recognition that teaching and social work need to be seen to be professional.

In examining these five methods it is hoped that this text has helped in that direction.

References

CCETSW, *Research and Practice*, 1980.

Entwistle, N.J. 'Labelling and Libelling students', *Times Higher Educational Supplement*, 29 March 1974, pp. 13-14.

Hayward, C., *A Fair Assessment*, CCETSW Study 2, 1979.

Millham, S., Bullock, R. and Hosie, K., *Learning to Care*, Gower Publishing Company, 1980.

Morrison, A. and McIntyre, D., *Teachers and Teaching*, Penguin, 1975.

Warnock, *Special Educational Needs*, HMSO, 1978.

Index